"Riggenbach has combined his understanding of CBT with a broad range of clinical experience with patients experiencing a number of different life problems. Using many clear clinical examples, he moves easily between theory, conceptualization, treatment planning, and the application of CBT techniques. The result is a clinically valuable book that is useful for the experienced therapist or the novice therapist wanting to gain expertise in CBT. It is well-written, user-friendly, and filled with the information and ideas that can only come from an expert clinician."

Arthur Freeman, EdD, ScD, ABPP
Executive Program Director of Clinical Psychology, Midwestern University

"A valuable and practical guide that will show you how to use the CBT model and techniques to help clients with a variety of problems including self-esteem issues, stress, codependency, depression and anxiety. Clear, accessible and easy-to-read, this workbook presents each problem in terms of the characteristic thinking patterns, feelings and behaviors of the client. Effective and practical tools including reproducible forms and handouts are provided to facilitate healing. Whether you are familiar with or new to CBT, this workbook is highly recommended."

John Ludgate, Ph.D,
Founding Fellow of the Academy of Cognitive Therapy and author of *Heal Yourself:
A CBT Approach to Reducing Therapist Distress and Increasing Therapeutic Effectiveness*

The CBT Toolbox
A Workbook for Clients and Clinicians

By
**Jeff Riggenbach,
Ph.D., LPC**

Copyright © 2013 by Jeff Riggenbach
Published by
PESI Publishing and Media
PESI, Inc
3839 White Ave
Eau Claire, WI 54703

Cover Design: Amy Rubenzer
Edited by: Marietta Whittlesey
Page Design: Matt Pabich & Amy Rubenzer

Printed in the United States of America

ISBN: 978-1-936-12830-3

PESI Publishing & Media
www.pesipublishing.com

Jeff Riggenbach, Ph.D., LPC,
is a licensed professional counselor in the state of
Oklahoma. He is currently on staff at Brookhaven
Psychiatric Hospital and Clinic in Tulsa where he
coordinates their Borderline Personality Disorder
Program as well as their Mood and Anxiety
Disorders Treatment Program. Dr. Riggenbach
trained at The Beck Institute of Cognitive
Therapy and Research in Philadelphia, and lectures
nationally and internationally on topics related
to CBT and personality dysfunction. He is a
Diplomat of the Academy of Cognitive Therapy, a
member of The Beck Institute's Speaker's Bureau,
and has served as a site director for an international
outcome trial treating individuals with BPD.

Dr. Riggenbach is known for bridging the gap
between academia, research findings and day-to-day
clinical practice, and his seminars on DBT, CBT,
and Schema-Focused Cognitive Therapy receive
the highest evaluations in terms of clinical utility as
well as entertainment value.

TABLE OF CONTENTS

Chapter 1 **CBT 101**

One day, while on my way to a speaking engagement, there was some confusion with my plane ticket, which had been purchased some three months in advance. After doing some scrambling, the airline accommodated me and got me in one of the last seats on the flight. I was flying on a plane that had two seats on one side of the aisle and three seats on the other side. Having received one of the last tickets on the entire flight, of course I was assigned one of those highly coveted middle seats. Not a petite individual myself, I was less than thrilled to discover my assigned seat was in between two clinically obese people!

There I was, jammed in between these two individuals with no room to move at all. It didn't take long before the person on my right began sweating profusely. With no room to move, her sweat began dripping on me—if you fly much, you know they don't start circulating the air until the plane begins taxiing toward the runway for takeoff. Then we had some minor mechanical difficulty, so I was sandwiched in, no room to move at all … and, as if it couldn't get any worse, a lady in front of me started changing her baby's diaper! I was jammed in there, no room to move at all, accumulating sweat by the moment, with a horrible stench emanating throughout the cabin. Any guesses how I felt? Wouldn't everyone in that situation feel the same way? As I turned my head, I noticed the lady on my left smiling, laughing, and saying things like, "Goo goo, ga ga" and playing with the baby through the space between the seats. She was trying to help the mother out. She was trying to get the baby to stop screaming. If you had taken a picture of this woman's face, you might have guessed she was having the time of her life! Although she was in virtually the same situation as I was, she was experiencing it in a much more enjoyable way. Why? Because she was obviously having different thoughts!

This happened to me fairly recently, and I often share this or similar stories at my seminars. Although it has a bit of a humorous element, it also illustrates, in practical terms, the role one's thought process plays in influencing emotions and, ultimately, impacting one's experience, illustrating the cognitive model of psychotherapy, also known as cognitive behavioral therapy (CBT).

CBT (Beck, 2011) is based on the principle that thoughts influence feelings, feelings influence actions, and actions influence our results, or life circumstances. In other words, situations don't *make* us feel certain ways. People don't *make* us feel certain ways. It's how we interpret (or think about) situations or things people say or do that influences how we feel.

So a simplified, linear version of the general model of CBT looks like this:

Event ➡ Thoughts ➡ Feelings ➡ Actions ➡ Results

We experience some kind of an event in life (often referred to as a trigger). How we think about, process, or interpret that event will affect what type of emotions we experience *and* how intensely we feel them. Feelings often influence actions. And how we choose to respond influences the outcome, or the circumstances in which we find ourselves. You may hear more in-depth explanations, variations, or nuances of this model, but these are the basics you need to understand to get you started.

Let's start with a few commonly asked questions about CBT:

Where in this sequence can I intervene directly to impact the end result?

Do I choose or can I influence events in my life?
Sometimes. Sometimes we put ourselves in situations that make us vulnerable to certain triggers. For example, we choose whom we date, whom we marry, whether we go to certain parties or hang out with certain people, whether we stay at a job or leave it, whether or not to engage in substance use. And sometimes we do not.

We don't choose our parents, our siblings, the situations our caretakers put us in when we are young, who is driving on the road when we are, or natural disasters. We have a say regarding some of the events (triggers) we experience, and others are completely out of our control.

Do I choose my thoughts and feelings?

To answer this question, let's try a brief exercise. Close your eyes. Picture a giraffe. Can you do it? Picture a snowflake. Can you see it? Picture yourself in your best friend's house. Can you conjure up these images? Of course you can. *Now* feel enraged. Just feel it. Can you do it? What did you have to do to feel enraged? You had to *think* about something that would get you there. Maybe you thought about an ex. Some of you perhaps thought about an issue that ticks you off. Patients will often think about an abusive situation or "the jerk that cut me off in traffic." Regardless of *what* you thought, the point is that it's almost impossible to command our feelings. Has anyone ever said to you something like, "Oh, come on, there's no need to be depressed—you have so much to be thankful for"? How many times has that been helpful? How many of you have said, "Oh, thanks for the feedback—I'll now choose to be happy"? It is worth noting that well-meaning people can say hurtful and invalidating things. Sometimes people want to help but just don't know how. The point here is that we typically don't have direct access to our feelings; we generally only have access to our feelings through our thoughts. So if you have been frustrated when someone told you to just "be happy," you're not alone! However, if feelings are influenced by thoughts—and as our exercise just illustrated, we do have some control over our thought life—then we do have the power to influence our feelings by learning to slowly retrain the way we think. Does that mean we choose all of our thoughts? Absolutely not. We all have thoughts that "just come." Sometimes we know exactly where they came from, and sometimes it seems as though they came "out of left field." The clinical term for these is *automatic thoughts*. We all have these thoughts, some of which we will never be able to keep ourselves from experiencing. However, although we don't always have a choice about whether these thoughts "appear," once they do, we can get better at increasing our awareness, paying attention to them, and working to change them through the tools this workbook teaches!

What is the difference between thoughts and feelings?

Thoughts are not feelings. A lot of people say things like, "I felt like he was scheming against me." That is not a feeling—it is a thought. That type of thought often leads to feelings of *fear*, *hurt*, or *betrayal*. We teach our patients, "If it's a full sentence, it's a thought." Feelings are one word and are expressions of emotion. Examples include *angry, sad, mad, happy, excited, fearful, anxious, overwhelmed, panicked,* and *annoyed.* Some people do not get the importance of this, but for a person to learn to use the tools this workbook provides, it is important to understand the difference. As we discuss in the paragraphs that follow, it is the *content* of our thoughts that determines what *types of emotions* we feel.

Is rational thinking the same thing as positive thinking?

No. There are a lot of different terms used to describe unhealthy thinking (e.g., *irrational, dysfunctional, maladaptive, distorted*), but positive thinking focuses only on the positive. Rational thinking focuses on probability, likelihood, patterns, and evidence. So there is such a thing as rational thinking that is negative. The reality is that there are a lot of negative aspects to life that require acceptance. There is also a sort of positive thinking that is irrational. In extreme forms, this may be called delusional thinking. It is often helpful to focus on positives but not to ignore the reality of negatives in our lives. Several "tools" have been designed to help you in this process and are discussed in this chapter.

Do we choose our actions?

Occasionally, this question gets some people fired up. This book provides a tool or two to help you in this area. But the short answer is that we almost always choose our actions. (There are a couple of clinical conditions in which a person literally does things outside of his or her awareness, but these are rare.) Some people say things like, "He made me do it" or "I didn't have a choice" or "what about fight or flight?" Some decisions are made instantaneously, and the thought process behind them is less conscious, but in order to determine whether thinking was involved, helpful questions to ask include:

- Would it have been possible to NOT do the action in that situation?
- Is there someone else in my life who would have reacted differently?

Do I choose my results?

Our actions *influence* our results. *Influence* is an important word to understand, because it doesn't mean *dictate*. Thus, it is not accurate to say we *choose* our results. It is possible that when we make healthy decisions, bad things still happen. It is also possible to make a certain number of poor choices and get away with it. But, generally speaking, the more healthy choices you make, the better chance you have of a positive outcome, and the more unhealthy choices you make, the better chance you have of running into trouble in some area of your life (relationally, occupationally, financially, legally, etc).

Another important principle of CBT is that all behavior makes sense. That is, we all come to think the way we do for specific reasons—all behavior serves a purpose. However, the ideas we have learned over the years aren't always healthy—some may have worked in one setting but not in another. Some may have worked at one point in life but not anymore. So, ideas that don't work aren't necessarily crazy, irrational ideas. They helped at one point in one setting in life but are no longer helpful. The idea, then, is to identify ways of thinking that are in some way distorted or dysfunctional and test and modify them over time. The clinical term for changing the way you think is *cognitive restructuring*. The good news is that over time, anything that is learned can be unlearned. Notice the phrase *over time*. It took your whole life thus far to come to think the way you do. So, retraining the way you think takes time. CBT is not "don't worry, be happy" therapy. It takes a critical look at how you process information, attempts to test and modify this over time, and eventually helps you change the way you think and respond to life circumstances.

How can two different people go through the exact same life event and come out with a vastly different experience?

People are different. We have each gone through unique experiences in life that shape how we view things. These experiences help create what are often called *core beliefs* or *schemas*. Although technically, these two terms don't have exactly the same meaning, this workbook uses the terms interchangeably. Our definition for both is "a mental filter that guides how people interpret events." Judy Beck, the director of The Beck Institute for Cognitive Therapy, created a visual of a schema that looks like this:

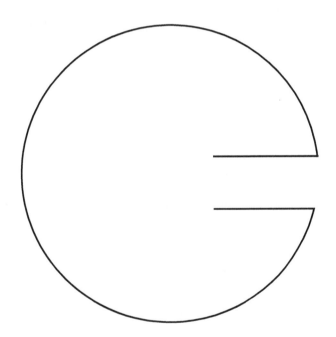

It is thought that the most common negative belief that the average person has about himself or herself is a belief that he or she is a failure. Picture this imaginary structure in your brain.

When someone who has this belief has experiences in life that are consistent with this theme, it reinforces that the belief is true. These experiences can be represented in a schema diagram by rectangles. Examples might include the following:

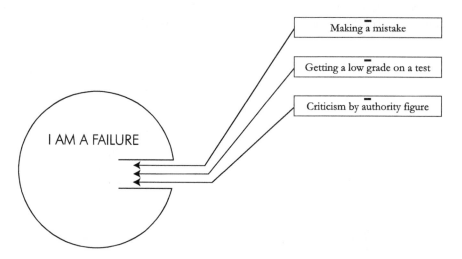

Conversely, when someone with this belief experiences something that is contradictory to his or her core beliefs, we might represent these with triangles.

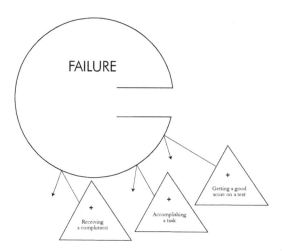

When life events are inconsistent with one's particular belief, the person often comes up with some reason the experiences don't "count." This is how low self-esteem is maintained. This book provides tools designed to help with this.

Another way to think about beliefs is that they make us pay attention to some things more than other things. Although these beliefs are typically unconscious, we can, through awareness exercises, become more in tune with them and how they are being reinforced. Politicians use beliefs purposefully to manipulate the public and call the process "spin."

As an example of the ways in which beliefs shape how we interpret events, I often remember the television commercial featuring Michael Jordan in which he said, "I missed more than 9000 shots, lost 300 games, missed 26 game-winning opportunities the team trusted me with .... I have failed over and over and over in my life ...." Would we view him as a "failure?" Of course not. He is the undisputed best player to ever play the game of opposite, healthy beliefs, but almost always, that. Our filters give meaning to events by shaping how we interpret them and what we pay attention to.

Identifying what specific beliefs or "filters" you have is an important part of recovery, as these are what shape how you respond to life situations. The following (AT Beck, 1987, J. Young, 1993)is not an exhaustive list, but some common themes this workbook addresses are:

Failure: The belief that one isn't good enough, can't do anything right, is a loser.

Approval seeking/Unlovable or unlikable: The belief that one is not likable or lovable, that nobody cares about him or her, and that he or she can't make or keep friends or romantic relationships, and he or she is bothered by these thoughts. If you are a "people-pleaser," this is the belief that is involved.

Helplessness: The belief that one can't cope—with a particular situation or with life in general. This core belief leads to feelings of inadequacy and anxiety.

Worthlessness/Defectiveness: The belief that one has no value or is unworthy … or is "damaged goods." For some people, these beliefs feel similar, and for others, they are different.

Abandonment: The belief that significant others in one's life will leave or won't be there for him or her and that he or she will not be able to tolerate being alone. People with this belief may go to extreme measures to keep from being alone.

Mistrust: The belief that others are untrustworthy, out to get one, or otherwise not looking out for one's best interest. This is a core belief that leads people to become overly suspicious or outright paranoid.

Vulnerability: There are different versions of this belief, as it can show up in different areas of life, but in general, this is the belief that one is unsafe and in some way (relationally, medically, financially) overly susceptible to being hurt. People with this belief interpret events in life as more threatening than they really are.

Emotional inhibition: The belief that one must inhibit one's emotions—not speak up or not share thoughts or feelings—because to do so would be unacceptable or harmful in some way.

Emotional deprivation: The belief that one will not get emotional needs met, so he or she often doesn't try. Some people with this belief will say, "I don't have needs," "Your needs are more important than mine," or "It's weak to have needs."

Subjugation: This belief is related to control. Some people believe they must turn control over their lives to others, while others make efforts not to be controlled or controlling. If you have "control issues," this belief is involved.

Entitlement: People with this filter believe that they are special or in some way better than or more deserving than others. Often, this serves to cover up an underlying insecurity (defectiveness, emotional deprivation beliefs): People who feel insecure but do not want to be seen as fragile put on a "tough guy" or "tough girl" facade. However, some were raised with no limits growing up and really do view themselves as better than others.

Punishment: The belief that one deserves to be punished. Punishment can be directed toward self or others. Our society has become quite litigious due to this belief. There are some psychiatric patients and inmates who just can't wait to file a grievance. Sadistic, masochistic, and self-harming behaviors may also be products of this belief.

Insufficient self-control: The belief that produces the cognition, "I have to have it now." People with this belief in the "heat of the moment" believe that they have no self-control, no ability to restrain themselves or delay gratification. Impulsive substance abuse, sexual promiscuity, binge eating, or temper tantrums and shopping sprees may be products of this belief.

It is important to remember that core beliefs *feel* true, but just because they feel true doesn't mean they are. That is what core beliefs do: They make things that aren't facts feel like facts. Patients will often say, "I feel like such a loser," to which I will always reply, "Just because you feel like a loser doesn't mean you are one." Labeling beliefs as beliefs and not accepting them as global facts about ourselves is a vital part of getting better. This book contains tools designed to help you in this process of testing your beliefs, but it is of fundamental importance to keep an open mind and recognize that things can feel true that aren't. CBT is not for closed-minded people.

Different beliefs produce different types of thoughts. Alcoholics Anonymous has a term called *stinkin' thinkin*, or basically, thoughts that don't serve us well. CBT has a more accurate and specific way of categorizing these types of thoughts that are unhelpful and lead to different types of feelings. In other words, every time you feel angry, there is a certain type of thought you are experiencing. Every time you feel anxiety, there are certain types of thoughts going through your mind.

Following is a list of types of thought processes that don't serve people well, known as cognitive distortions. There are many versions of the list floating around out there using different terminology. Much of this can be attributed to the work of David Burns (1999) in his initial work, *The Feeling Good Handbook*, which does an excellent job of breaking down in every day terms the work of Drs. Aaron Beck, Albert Ellis, and others who are considered pioneers of this field. The list that follows the diagram is my adaptation from Burns' book. Every chapter in this book refers to this list and teaches you tools based on it.

Cognitive Distortions

Thoughts: You interpret events with a series of thoughts that flow through your mind.

The World: A series of positive, neutral, and negative events.

Mood: Your feelings are influenced by your thoughts.

Your emotions result from the way you *look* at things. Before you can experience any feeling, you must process it with your mind and give it meaning. The way that you *understand* what is happening influences how you *feel* about it. To the degree that your thinking about a given event is biased in any way, your feelings may be that much more intense, which will make it that much harder to act in a way that is helpful.

What follows are 10 misperceptions, which we will call cognitive distortions, that form the basis for your emotional difficulties (adapted from Burns, 1990).

1. Rationalization. In an attempt to protect yourself from hurt feelings, you create excuses for events in life that don't go your way or for poor choices you make. We might call these *permission-giving statements* that give ourselves or someone else permission to do something that is in some way unhealthy.

2. Overgeneralization. You categorize different people, places, and entities based on your own experiences with each particular thing. For example, if you have been treated poorly by men in the past, "all men are mean," or if your first wife cheated on you, "all women are unfaithful." By overgeneralizing, you miss out on experiences that don't fit your particular stereotype. This is the distortion on which all of those "isms" (e.g., racism, sexism) are based.

3. All-or-nothing thinking. This refers to a tendency to see things in black and white categories with no consideration for gray. You see yourself, others, and often the whole world in only positive or negative extremes rather than considering that each may instead have both positive and negative aspects. For example, if your performance falls short of perfect, you see yourself as a total failure. If you catch yourself using extreme language (best ever, worst, love, hate, always, never), this is a red flag that you may be engaging in all-or-nothing thinking. Extreme thinking leads to intense feelings and an inability to see a "middle ground" perspective or feel proportionate moods.

4. Discounting the positive. You reject positive experiences by insisting that they "don't count" for some reason or another. In this way, you can maintain a negative belief that is contradicted by your everyday experiences. The terms *mental filter* and *selective abstraction* basically describe the same process.

5. Fortune telling. You anticipate that things will turn out badly and feel convinced that your prediction is already an established fact based on your experiences from the past. Predicting a negative outcome before any outcome occurs leads to anxiety and other negative emotions. A lot of people call this process the "what ifs."

6. Mind reading. Rather than predicting future events, engaging in this distortion involves predicting that you know what someone else is thinking when in reality you don't. This distortion commonly occurs in communication problems between romantic partners.

7. Should statements. You place false or unrealistic expectations on yourself or others, thereby setting yourself up to feel angry, guilty, or disappointed. Words and phrases such as *ought to, must, has to, needs to,* and *supposed* to are indicative of "should" thinking.

8. Emotional reasoning. You assume that your negative feelings reflect the way things really are. "I feel it, therefore it must be true."

9. Magnification. You exaggerate the importance of things, blowing them way out of proportion. Often, this takes the form of fortune telling and/or mind reading to an extreme. This way of thinking may also be referred to as *catastrophizing* or *awfulizing*.

10. Personalization. You see yourself as the cause of some external negative event for which, in fact, you were not primarily responsible. You make something about you that is not about you and get your feelings hurt.

Now that you have the basic CBT framework, you are ready to learn specific "tools" to add to your therapeutic toolbox that will equip you on you journey toward recovery!

HOW TO USE THIS WORKBOOK

The following "tools" are skills and activities you can add to your toolbox of resources to be better equipped to deal with problems that may come your way. Some people may struggle in all of these areas, while other users may find only one or two chapters to be relevant to them. For example, some may struggle only with depression or anxiety, whereas others may struggle with toxic relationships or codependency.

You may notice the same tools show up in different chapters. The reason for this is that even though the *process* is the same, the *content* is different. For instance, events that trigger low self-esteem may be very different from the events that trigger anger, and although the process of identifying and changing thoughts and testing beliefs is the same, the types of beliefs involved with different problems differ. In other words, the types of thoughts that need to be changed to combat depression are different than the types of thoughts that perpetuate anxiety. So if you find that a tool in Chapter 8 appears to be the same as a tool you've worked with in Chapter 3, it's important not to assume, "I've already done that in a previous chapter." Even though the questions in the tool may sound similar, your answers will probably be different because it is a different problem you are addressing. Also, while in each chapter the first 14 tools look similar, the last several tools are different and are specifically related to the problem area discussed in that chapter.

Chapter 2 **Self-Esteem**

COMMON BELIEFS

- I am undeserving.
- I am unlovable.
- I am defective.
- I am vulnerable.
- I am a loser
- I am weak
- I am stupid
- I am not good enough
- I am ugly

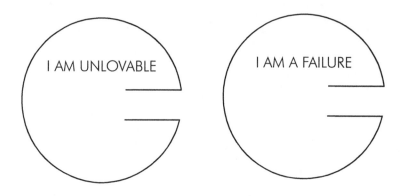

COMMON DISTORTIONS

- Discounting of the positive
- Selective abstraction
- Mental filter

COMMON AUTOMATIC THOUGHTS

- "Because I failed this project, I'll never succeed."
- "Because I didn't do it perfectly, it's no good at all."
- "If I can't be perfect, I might as well not even start."
- "Because I'm overweight, I don't matter as much as others who are in shape."
- "If I let them get to know me, people won't like me."

COMMON FEELINGS

- Inadequacy
- Sadness
- Hopelessness
- Anxiety

COMMON BEHAVIORS

- Underachieving in work
- Underachieving in school
- Choosing poor relationships

Many people would describe themselves as having "low self-esteem" all the time. But it is worse for some people than for others. Even though many think of themselves as having low self esteem "all the time," the reality is that most people have times when they may feel better or worse than others about themselves but just don't recognize those times.

One helpful exercise involves paying close attention to what life events trigger these feelings of low self-worth. Triggers can be people, places, or things. Sometimes, they are more obvious, such as someone yelling at you in the same way a parent did. Other triggers are more subtle, such as a song on the radio that reminds you of a time in your life or passing someone in the mall wearing a perfume that reminds you of a person or a situation. Take a few minutes to answer the following questions that may give you a window into your low self-esteem triggers.

I usually notice my low self-esteem most when _____

I seem to feel worst about myself when _____

The last time I noticed feeling this way was _____

Themes in times I feel poorly about myself include _____

Things that seem to happen right before I feel this way are _____

My low self-esteem triggers are:

1.

2.

3.

4.

5.

Some people are very good at expressing their feelings. Others have difficulty recognizing feelings, giving names to feelings, or even recognizing that they have feelings at all. The following "Feelings Face Sheet" is often helpful for aiding people in identifying what feelings they are actually having. Using the face sheet as your guide, pick out several emotions that seem to describe best what you experience when you are feeling low self-esteem. If this "feelings face sheet" is helpful, many versions of it exist as well and can be located at multiple sources.

Feelings Log

Type of Feeling	Mon	Tues	Wed	Thurs	Fri	Sat	Sun
Happy							
Sad							
Excited							
Angry							
Irritated							
Frustrated							
Proud							
Regretful							
Disgusted							
Excited							
Guilty							
Ashamed							
Anxious							
Confident							
Resentful							
Gloomy							
Fearful							
Scared							
Panicked							
Grateful							
Loved							
Envious							
Jealous							
Compassionate							
Affectionate							

My low self-esteem feelings are:

1.

2.

3.

4.

5.

Some therapists may use the term *irrational thoughts.*(Ellis, 1975). Others prefer the term *dysfunctional thoughts* or *maladaptive thoughts.*(AT Beck, 1987) The advantage of thinking of thoughts as dysfunctional is recognizing that thoughts that were functional or helpful in one setting may become dysfunctional or hurtful in other settings. For instance, someone who grew up in an abusive family might have learned through experience that, "If I speak up, somebody gets hit or yelled at, or someone leaves, so it's best that I just never speak up." Now, if someone really did get hurt every time he opened his mouth, it would be adaptive to keep his mouth shut. But, if that person adopts that way of thinking ("It's best that I just keep my mouth shut") even after he has grown up and left that home, it is not functional or adaptive and will not lead to effective outcomes. Thus, what is functional in one setting is not necessarily helpful in other contexts. Other professionals may use the term *distorted thinking*. This is the term this workbook uses. Distorted thoughts might be defined as any thoughts that in get in the way of our feeling and behaving in healthy manners.

The following questions are designed to help you identify your distorted thoughts specifically related to low self-esteem:

When _____ (trigger; see Tool 1 in this chapter) **happens,**
and I feel _____ (feelings; see Tool 2 in this chapter), **what am I usually telling myself?**

If I were in a cartoon, what would the bubble above my head be saying?

If there were a tape recorder in my head recording my every thought, what would it be saying when someone pushed "play?"

Example

I felt ...	...because I thought...
Sad	I thought this project means that I will never amount to anything and I am a complete failure.
Angry	He should be more fair.
Relieved	At least I won't have to put up with that anymore.

Thoughts/Feelings Awareness Log

I felt ...	...because I thought...

Most people develop a set of standard "Go-To" coping skills when they feel poorly about themselves. Perhaps you have heard the phrase "on autopilot," referring to just falling back on the same old skills that in some way feel comfortable but usually don't help. Typically, these behaviors "worked" in the past but no longer work in the present. Also, some may continue to "work" in the short term but make problems worse in the long term. For example, alcohol, drugs, promiscuous sex, spending, or workaholism are methods people use to avoid feeling negative feelings about themselves. Before figuring out healthy skills to use when these feelings creep up, it is often useful to generate a list of what we have been trying that has *NOT* been working.

The last time I felt my low self-esteem, I _____

Other things I have done in the past in an attempt to cope that have in some way hurt me are:

Some of my "go to"/"autopilot" coping skills are:

1.

2.

3.

4.

5.

As Tool 4 touched on, things that worked in the past don't always work in the present, and things that work in the present in the short term don't always work in the long term. Some people have little to no awareness as to how their past coping choices have impacted their present life circumstances. Others fully recognize that their present choices may cause future consequences but continue to choose that "quick feel-good" choice regardless. One tool that often helps motivate people to change is to take a close look at how their past behaviors have contributed to present undesirable situations. When considering consequences for autopilot behaviors, keep in mind that consequences can take many forms. Areas to consider in your life may include relationships, mood, physical health, financial circumstances, spiritual life, and occupational satisfaction, to name just a few. Spend a few minutes seeing if you can make some of these connections.

Example

Autopilot Coping Skill (from Tool 4)	Current or Past Negative Consequences
Upset over comment Sally made, so spent $500 impulsively	Short on rent $
Yelled at best friend	She hasn't spoken to me in 2 weeks. Kind of feel like she deserved it, but I miss her and I am lonely.

Awareness of Consequences Log

Autopilot Coping Skill (from Tool 4)	Current or Past Negative Consequences

Maybe you've heard it said that "Change = Insight + Action." While it is true that many people never develop insight into their unhealthy behaviors, it's also true that many people do develop insight into their unhealthy behaviors but never take action to change them! Perhaps you have also heard Albert Einstein's definition of insanity: *doing the same thing over and over again expecting a different result!* For instance, some people recognize that their romantic partner "picker" is broken but continue to select unhealthy men or women to be with. Millions of Americans now recognize that smoking has many health hazards but refuse to quit. The reality is, if we want things to get better in our lives, we have to be willing to try something different! Fortune telling gets in the way and convinces us "this won't work because…." But the truth is that until we try, we won't know. We may try a new skill and it doesn't work either, but at least we tried. We can now add it to our list of skills we already know don't work, and move on to try something else. It is kind of like trying on new shoes—if one pair doesn't fit, no harm done. We just put them in the pile that won't work for us and keep trying. Refer to your list of coping skills and pick some things you are willing to try next time you feel your low self-esteem about to influence you to fall into unhealthy autopilot mode.

Some things I will try the next time I feel horrible about myself are:

1.

2.

3.

4.

5.

6.

7.

8.

9.

10.

In the same way that recognizing but continuing unhealthy behaviors rarely gets us far along in recovery, recognizing distorted thoughts but not challenging them also keeps us stuck. Recognizing and identifying these thoughts is an important first step, but if we don't rigorously challenge them too, we will continue to suffer those same horrible feelings we have about ourselves, which will, in turn, make it more difficult not to revert to those autopilot behaviors. Challenging distorted thoughts doesn't always make them go away, but it can put up enough of a "fight" that feelings aren't quite so intense, and thus it may be at least slightly easier to use some of the skills you identified in Tool 6. Utilize the following *thought log* to attempt to *challenge* or generate some more *rational responses* to the distorted thoughts you identified in Tool 3.

Example

Distorted Thought	Rational Response
Because I failed this project, I will never amount to anything and I am a complete failure.	I didn't do my best, but I didn't completely fail. Even though I wouldn't classify this as a success, I have succeeded at many other projects. Everybody has bad days. It's not fair to judge myself with a harsher standard than others. I have had other successes outside of work as well, so its not fair to say that I am a complete failure. I already have a decent job for someone my age. And it's possible I will have further successes in the future.

Thought Log

Distorted Thought	Rational Response

As mentioned in Chapter 1, *core beliefs* are deeply ingrained beliefs that we have in different areas of life (self, others, and the world). They serve as "filters" through which we process information. Because we all have had different life experiences, our filters are unique. It is because of these filters that we may perceive things differently, so that two people can go through the same event and come out of it with a different experience. Filters contribute to different thoughts, feelings, and responses. One tool that can help identify core beliefs is called the *downward arrow* technique (J. Beck, 2005). This technique asks us to take a thought and continue to ask, "What would that mean about us if it were true?" until we get at the core belief at the bottom of the distorted thought. Note the following example and then try one on your own. Many people need a therapist's help to assist with this for a period of time.

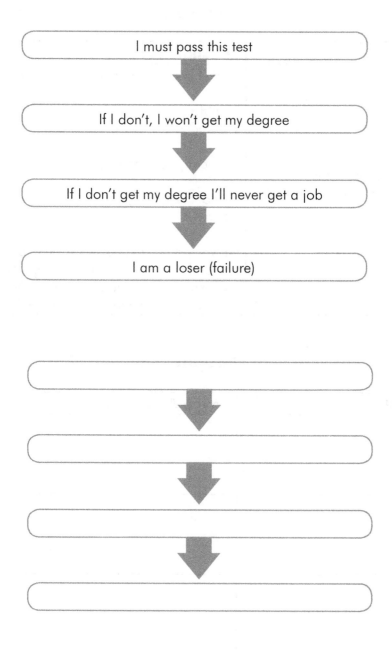

When hearing all this talk of maladaptive or unhealthy beliefs, some people ask, "Aren't there any healthy beliefs?" The reality is that we all have healthy beliefs, but the focus is usually on our unhealthy beliefs because those are the ones that are responsible for the difficulties we are facing. It's similar to when we take our car into the shop: The mechanic never tells us about the 300 and some things that *are working*. He tells us about the one or two that are not, because that is why we had to bring the car in to begin with. Similarly, in therapy, the focus is often on the unhealthy beliefs, but *the reality is that beliefs come in pairs*. For every unhealthy belief, we all have an opposite, healthy belief. For instance, if you identified a self-belief that says, *"I am a failure,"* you may want to identify your opposite healthy belief as something like, *"I can succeed."* Take a few minutes, and for each unhealthy belief you identified using Tool 7, think about how you might want to phrase the opposite of that. Keep in mind that it is helpful to keep beliefs flexible, such as *"can succeed"* rather than *"am always successful."* You may note that these beliefs are represented by a similar "pac-man" type figure, but have an opening a "triangle" could fit into.

My Beliefs

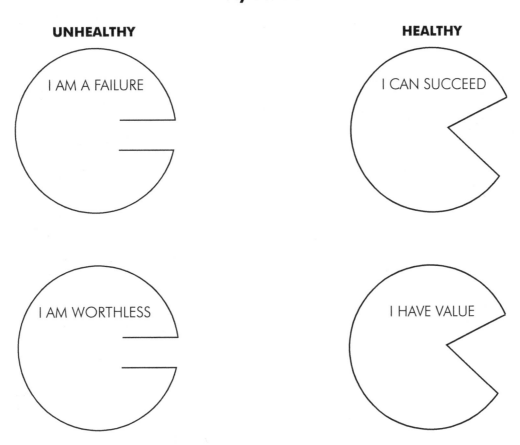

© J Beck, 2005. Adapted from *Cognitive Therapy for Challenging Problems* and used with permission.

My Beliefs

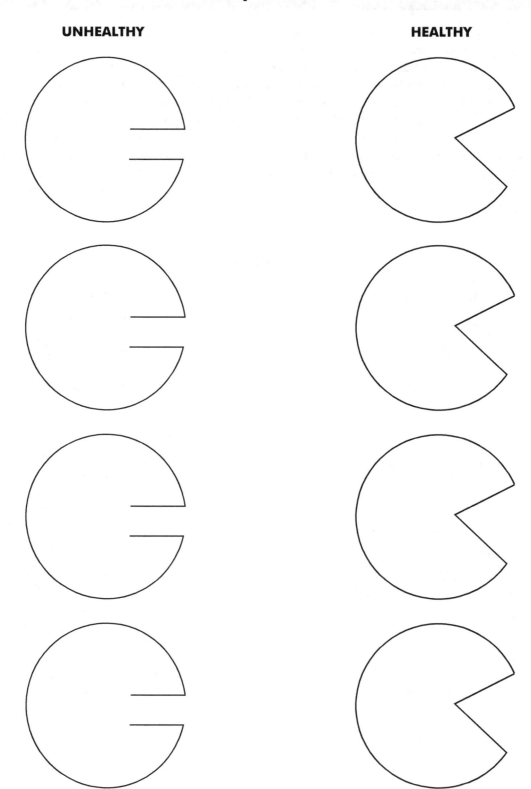

Just because we believe something doesn't mean we believe it 100 percent. For instance there are people who are convinced (a 100 percent belief) that there is life on other planets. There are people who are certain there is not (a 0 percent belief). Others may believe it is *possible*, but not likely (maybe a 10 percent belief). Similarly, some people believe they are a failure 100 percent of the time and successful 0 percent of the time. Others may see themselves as a failure 70 percent and as successful 30 percent. The strength of our beliefs significantly influences how often we feel certain emotions and how strongly we experience them. Take a few minutes and try to assign a strength to each healthy and unhealthy belief. Usually, the easiest way is to use percentages so the total for unhealthy and healthy beliefs equals 100 percent.

Example

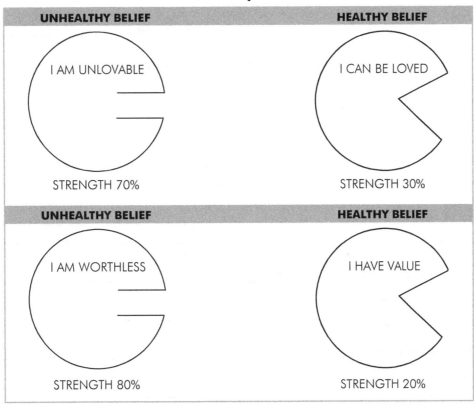

Rating the Strength of My Beliefs

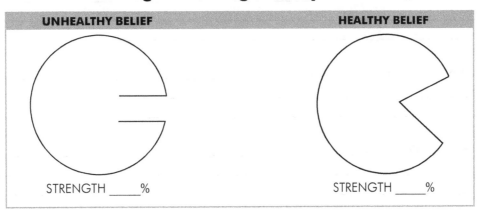

Leslie Sokol, a faculty member at the Beck Institute, compares a belief to a tabletop. In the same way that tabletops need legs to hold them up, beliefs need legs or "evidence" to support them. *"Evidence"* is in quotation marks, because different people *count* evidence differently. For instance, some people who believe in aliens may have heard the same stories (information) as people who do not, but for various reasons, one person "counts" the stories as "evidence" and the other does not. The same holds true for beliefs about ourselves. Anyone who has a failure belief about themselves, whether they realize it or not, has collected "evidence" that they have "counted" over the years to support that belief. This exercise can be a little more time consuming and emotionally draining than some of the previous ones but can be a powerful tool for recovery. The following questions may be helpful in reflecting back on different periods of life to uncover some of the experiences you counted as evidence to support your belief (legs to hold up your table). You may need assistance from your therapist to get the most out of this tool.

The first time I ever remember feeling _____ **[belief] was** _____

The people in my life who influenced me to feel that way were:

Family members _____

_____

Friends/Peers _____

_____

Other significant people _____

_____

Experiences during my elementary school years _____

_____

_____

Experiences during my junior high years _____

_____

_____

Experiences during my high school years _____

_____

_____

Experiences during my college/young adult years _____

_____

_____

Significant experiences since then _____

_____

_____

Use the exercise on the left to try to insert some of the "evidence" from your past that you have "counted" to support each belief.

Example

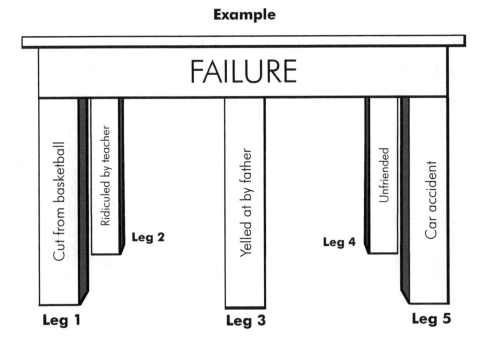

Evidence that I am a failure:

Leg 1: Cut from 8th grade basketball team

Leg 2: Ridiculed for science project by teacher

Leg 3: Father yelled at me in garage for mistake on construction project

Leg 4: Unfriended by classmate

Leg 5: Got into a car accident while texting and driving

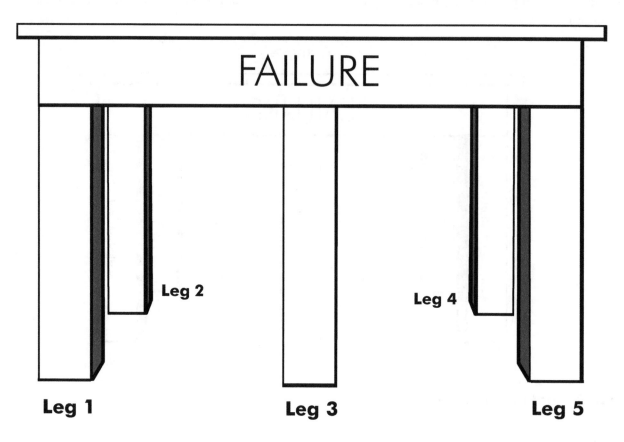

FAILURE

Leg 2

Leg 4

Leg 1

Leg 3

Leg 5

Evidence that I am a failure:

Leg 1:

Leg 2:

Leg 3:

Leg 4:

Leg 5:

Because of how our filters (beliefs) are set up, we often notice instances that support the unhealthy beliefs more than we notice those that may support our opposite, healthy beliefs; however, that "evidence" almost always exists as well. One valuable tool involves forcing ourselves to look back over those very same periods of life purposefully looking to see the evidence that supports our healthy beliefs. You may want to rely on family members or friends who were around during each period of life to help you "notice" such evidence. Even if they share things they see as "counting" that you don't think "should count" write them down anyway—a tool to help with that is provided later in the book!

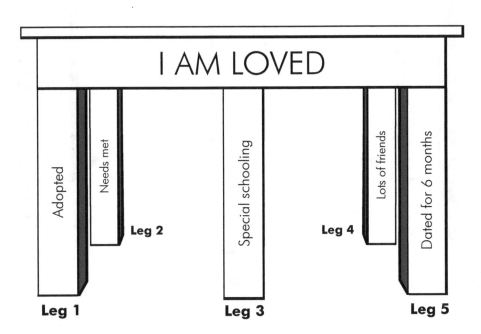

Evidence that I am loved:

Leg 1: My parents chose to adopt me.

Leg 2: I always had my basic needs met.

Leg 3: Mom enrolled me in a special school.

Leg 4: I had lots of friends in high school.

Leg 5: Sarah went out with me for 6 months.

Healthy Evidence Log

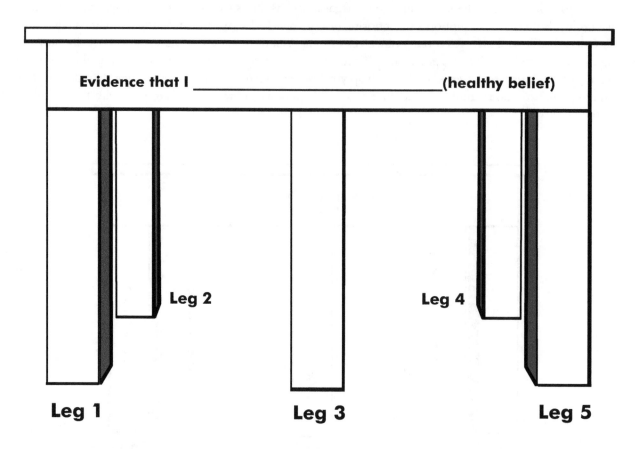

Evidence that I _____(healthy belief)

Leg 1

Leg 2

Leg 3

Leg 4

Leg 5

Leg 1:

Leg 2:

Leg 3:

Leg 4:

Leg 5:

Beliefs *mean* different things to different people. For instance, some people are working with the unhealthy belief that they are *worthless*. Perhaps an opposite healthy belief they are working to build is that they *have value*. People *value* things differently. Areas people may perceive as valuable or worthwhile include:

- Academic achievement/education
- Helping others
- Accomplishment
- Religious participation
- Kindness/Compassion
- Scientific exploration/advancement
- Time spent with family/friends
- Helping/Serving others
- Advocating for children
- Rescue/Protection of animals

Some people see certain things as valuable that others don't view as valuable at all. *Components* of the belief of *value* are different people. To build healthy beliefs, it is important to identify the *components* of your healthy belief.

Belief   **Components**

1.   **1.**

                                               2.

                                               3.

_____

2.   **1.**

                                               2.

                                               3.

_____

3.   **1.**

                                               2.

                                               3.

Another important tool for developing more healthy beliefs and thus becoming less reactive, is an *ongoing evidence log*. Whereas previous tools required you to review your life and look for "evidence" from the past, ongoing evidence logs ask you to be mindful of evidence in your everyday life. Since your unhealthy filters will naturally be pointing you toward negative evidence, it is often necessary to purposefully seek out positive evidence. "Purposefully seek out" doesn't mean "make it up" if it legitimately isn't there; rather, it means to try to pay attention to any evidence that legitimately may be present but was missed due to your negative filter. It is helpful to collect evidence for each belief with which you struggle, but it is recommended that you pick only one or two on which to focus at a given time.

Example
Evidence log that I can be liked/loved

Date	Evidence
3/12	Mom hugged me
3/13	Aunt sent me care package
3/16	Friend called to check on me
3/20	Got invited to a party
3/22	Scout leader said he appreciated me

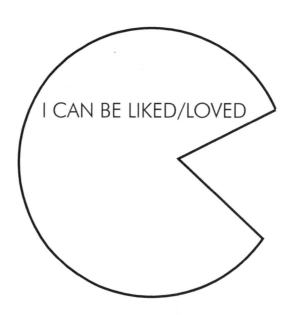

I CAN BE LIKED/LOVED

Evidence log that I can be liked/loved log

Date	Evidence

Self-esteem doesn't come from nowhere. We can't just repeat all day long positive affirmations that deep down we don't believe and expect self-esteem to appear overnight. Maybe you remember the line from *What About Bob?* in which Bill Murray's character, Bob Wiley, states, "I feel good, I feel great, I feel wonderful" over and over and over. Yet no matter how many times he recited those words, it was obvious that repetition alone didn't help him believe them. There are many myths surrounding self-esteem. Self-esteem can't be gained by any magic wand waving or mysterious tapping done in a therapy session. It has to come from somewhere. We have to do things that we consider worthwhile or possess qualities that we consider valuable and then *give ourselves credit* for possessing a particular skill or having a specific attribute. Step 1 is identifying the particular qualities, attributes, or skills that we have. The following exercise is fun for some people but quite difficult for others. Complete the following page, attempting to list for each letter of the alphabet one positive quality you possess or that can at least be demonstrated at times (Horton, 1998). Seek help from friends or family if you need to. Even if you find yourself hesitating on a particular quality or skill, force yourself to write it down anyway even if you don't believe it 100%. Later in the book, tools are provided to teach you skills for learning to believe it more.

A	**N**
B	**O**
C	**P**
D	**Q**
E	**R**
F	**S**
G	**T**
H	**U**
I	**V**
J	**W**
K	**X**
L	**Y**
M	**Z**

As we discussed in Chapter 1, hearing compliments can sometimes be difficult, particularly if they don't fit one of our beliefs. Perhaps even as you were writing some of your A-Z affirmations, that little voice in the back of your mind said, "Yes, but …" and came up with some reason for discounting the positive. One way to work on developing more healthy beliefs is by using the "add a but" tool. (J. Beck, 2005) The way this one works is that every time you hear a positive (triangle; see Chapter 1) and your distorted thinking kicks in and says, "Yes, but …," you write the "negative but" down but then add a "positive but"—something positive or healthy to counter the "negative but." You can do this with any of the attributes from your A-Z list, or you can try it with any compliments you receive from day to day. It is also important to re-rate your belief strength (see Tool 10 in this chapter) periodically to see if your beliefs about yourself (self-esteem) are changing.

Example

Positive Attribute/Skill	Discounting "But"	Add a "But"
I can be kind	I snapped at my husband last night	I also cooked him dinner and did his laundry

"But" Log

Positive Attribute/Skill	Discounting "But"	Add a "But"

Another part of self-esteem can come from knowing who we are. Some people are very certain of who they are, while for others, identity is a little less certain. Finding identity starts with answering the question, *"How do I define myself?"* Identity can be found in religious beliefs, personal strengths, occupations, hobbies, friends, causes we feel strongly about, gender, age, and our relationships to others, to name just a few. You have probably heard the expression "wearing a lot of hats." Consider for a few minutes the "hats" you wear. In doing work to develop identity, it can be helpful to think in terms of *I am, I have, I can,* and *I like.* Spend a few minutes and consider how you might answer these questions.

Example

I am … caring, loving, sensitive.

I have … a good family.

I can … knit/play golf

I like … cooking.

Now, in your own words:

I am _____

I have _____

I can _____

I like _____

Under each hat in the illustration below, write one of the ways you currently define yourself or a way that you may like to see yourself in the future. For instance, one participant's "hats" included being a *"niece, a sister, a friend, a Christian, a football player, a stamp collector, a chef, a secretary, and a movie goer."*

Adapted from DiClememte, 2004

Strengthening My Identity

The "hat" I most identify with is _____.

The one I least identify with is _____.

Three ways I can develop my identity as a _____ **are:**

1.

2.

3.

Contrary to popular belief, many perfectionists have low self-esteem. If you believe "If I can't do something perfectly, it's not worth doing at all," it is difficult to push yourself to do anything that you can later feel good about. This perfectionist mindset that keeps some from taking initiative also often keeps people from developing self-esteem. Many people take some good steps forward and *do* some good things or *possess* some admirable traits, but then that voice kicks in and says, "Since you didn't do it perfectly, it doesn't count" or "Since you aren't this way all the time, you don't get credit for it." Perfectionistic thoughts can keep us from recognizing when we really do make progress, because to the perfectionist, if it's not perfect, its no good at all, so it can't register as "evidence." Many of my patients carry a card with the phrase, "Progress not Perfection" as a way of reminding them that small steps of progress—not perfection—are the goal.

It can be helpful to be mindful each day of small steps you have taken forward. Also, it helps to ask yourself the question, "How was I in this area before I even started therapy?" This helps us remember what our "baseline" was and helps us see how far we've come. Emotional growth is a little like physical growth—you can't just stand there and look down at your feet when you're four years old and notice yourself growing, but each year when you go into the doctor, you've probably grown several inches, and one day you wake up and you are five-foot-six (or however tall you are). Similarly, emotional growth happens in small *increments*. So we must broaden our perspective to see how much we truly have grown. Use the following tool to note small progresses you make on a day-to-day basis.

Example

Issue	"Perfection"	Where I Started	Progress
Weight	110 lb	180 lb	170 lb

Things I can do this week to make progress toward my goal are:

1. Go to Weight Watchers

2. Buy health food for the week

3. Call Julie to walk together

Progress, not Perfection Charts

Issue	"Perfection"	Where I Started	Progress

Things I can do this week to make progress toward my goal are:

1.

2.

3.

Issue	"Perfection"	Where I Started	Progress

Things I can do this week to make progress toward my goal are:

1.

2.

3.

Issue	"Perfection"	Where I Started	Progress

Things I can do this week to make progress toward my goal are:

1.

2.

3.

Self-talk is a term often used to describe the dialogues we have in our minds, or "what we tell ourselves." We are quite aware of some self-talk, but much of it is less conscious. Tool 3 addressed identifying distorted thinking, and Tool 7 assisted us in challenging thoughts. Often people are able to identify their thinking and deal with thinking that is hurtful in major life situations but are unaware of the negative "tape" that plays almost unconsciously in response to certain events and sometimes on a regular basis. It is difficult to attempt to change thinking that we don't realize we are doing. Many people find it helpful to journal thoughts on a daily basis to increase their awareness as to what is going on in their own minds!

For some people, it is helpful to compare the battle of self-talk that occurs in their mind to those cartoons that have the angel on one shoulder and the devil on the other, with the angel representing rational or healthy self-talk and the devil representing distorted or unhealthy self-talk. Many people even find it helpful to name their "devil" character. Some just use descriptive terms, such as my "inner critic" or "critical parent" (a term from schema-focused cognitive therapy). A patient of mine once called it her "niggler," who was always "niggling" or poking or chiding her to believe negative things about herself that weren't true. A colleague of mine refers to that voice as "slick," that "smooth talker" (similar to the stereotypical used car salesman) who is always trying to deceive or trick someone. It may be helpful for you to try a version of this.

Not all distorted thinking is necessarily negative (some people have positive irrational thinking), but for people with low self-esteem and depression, distorted thinking often has a very negative quality. To work on increasing awareness of negative self-talk, it can be helpful to purposely pay attention to negative situations throughout the day and try to monitor things you might have been telling yourself at those particular times. The following tool can assist you with becoming more aware of negative self-talk:

Self-Talk Log

Date: _____

Event	Negative Self-Talk
The worst thing about today was:	Things my critical voice might have said when this happened:
The worst choice I made/one mistake I made today was:	What my critical voice might have said after I did it was:
One negative quality that I know I have that came out today was:	What my critical voice might have told me about myself when this came out was:

As you get better at recognizing what that critical voice is telling you, you can work to use challenging (Tool 7) on a more regular basis to gradually continue to improve your self-esteem.

All human beings are able to think more rationally when they are calm. On the flip side, it is more difficult for anyone to think rationally when they are "worked up" or have a "button pushed." So, it makes sense that these are the times our emotions often get the best of us and we make choices that are counterproductive. Wouldn't it be nice if we could think as rationally in the "heat of the moment" as we are able to after we calm down? The reality is that most people have difficulty thinking clearly under pressure. One tool that can assist us in doing better "in the heat of the moment" is flashcards. Coping cards are designed to help us *act* differently in such moments. Cognitive cue cards are designed to help us *think* differently in those situations. So the idea here is, in your calm moments, write down on a 3x5 note card what you believe you need to hear during the less-calm moments. A coping card always takes the following form:

Example

When I'm tempted to _____*Binge Eat*_____ (behavior from Tool 4),

I can (choices from Tool 6):

1. Take a walk.

2. Journal my feelings.

3. Take a soothing bath.

When I'm tempted to _____ (behavior from Tool 4),

I can (choices from Tool 6):

1. _____

2. _____

3. _____

A cognitive cue card does not list behaviors; rather, it takes triggers (Tool 1) and robs them of the negative meaning your critical voice is attempting to give them. Cue cards take the following form:

Just because _____ (trigger) doesn't mean _____ (critical message).

Challenge negative meaning with neutral or positive meaning.

Example

Cognitive Cue Card

Just because _I overate last night_ **doesn't mean** _I am a loser. I slipped this_

time, but I am making better choices than I was a month ago.

I know _my life has value_ **is true because** _I am smart, I'm loved by_

friends and family, and I care about people.

Cognitive Cue Card

Just because _____ **doesn't mean** _____

_____

I know _____ **is true because** _____

_____

Chapter 3 **Stress Management**

COMMON BELIEFS

- I am a failure
- I am unlovable
- I am worthless

COMMON DISTORTIONS

- Should statements (toward self, present tense)
- Personalization
- Fortune telling, mind reading

COMMON AUTOMATIC THOUGHTS

- "I have to get this house clean before the party."
- "I should be further on this project."
- "My boss is going to be ticked off at me if I fall behind."
- "We can't be late."
- "I have to have dinner on the table at a certain time!"

COMMON FEELINGS

- Stressed out
- Overwhelmed
- Pressured

COMMON BEHAVIORS

- Workaholic/overworking behaviors
- Perfectionistic behaviors
- Shutting down

It is true that some people are a little more "high strung" than others. So, some people appear to be in a nearly constant state of stress. But, as with self-esteem, there are times in life we feel more stressed than others and times we may feel less stressed. Again, triggers can be people, places, or things, and sometimes they are more obvious (e.g., an impending deadline) or preparing for company to come over or more subtle (e.g., a song reminds you of a bad experience).

Take a few minutes to answer the following questions that may give you a window into your triggers for stress:

I define stress as _____.

I seem to feel the most stressed out when _____.

The last time I noticed feeling this way was _____.

Themes of times I feel "worked up" include _____.

Things that seem to happen right before I feel this way are _____.

My triggers for stress are:

1.

2.

3.

4.

5.

Feelings of stress are very different than feelings of low self-esteem. Those who suffer from both will attest that they are both uncomfortable, but the "gut" feeling is not the same. Feelings often associated with stress often include *tension, stress, overwhelmed, anxious, worried* to name just a few. Some people feel a" sped up" feeling that is similar to hyperactivity.

Refer to your Face Sheet (Tool 2 in Chapter 2) to identify what feelings related to stress you frequently experience:

My stress-related feelings are:

1.

2.

3.

4.

5.

The following questions are designed to help you identify your distorted thoughts specifically related to stress. Remember, these thoughts will often fit in the category of "shoulding" or fortune-telling statements.

When _____ **(trigger; see Tool 1 in Chapter 2) happens,**

and I feel _____ **(feelings; see Tool 2 in Chapter 2), what am I usually telling myself?**

If I were in a cartoon, what would the bubble above my head be saying?

If there were a tape recorder in my head recording my every thought, what would it be saying when someone pushed "play?"

Example

I felt ...	... because I thought ...
Stressed	I must do well on this test.
Overwhelmed	This is too much, I can't do it.
Tense	She's probably going to yell at me any second now.

Thoughts/Feelings Awareness Log

I felt ...	... because I thought ...

"Autopilot" unhealthy coping skills used to cope with stress generally fit into one of a couple of categories. Many people choose skills designed to *avoid* stress-inducing triggers. Examples might include alcoholism and workaholism. People using these strategies may avoid feeling stress, but in their efforts, they create further problems for themselves. Others push themselves to do stressful things but then in an attempt to *soothe* themselves may engage in behaviors such as smoking pot or having careless sex.

Spend a few minutes trying to identify unhealthy behavior habits you may have developed in response to these feelings:

The last time I felt stressed out I did:

Other things I have done in the past in an attempt to cope that have in some way hurt me are:

Some of my "go-to"/"autopilot" coping skills are:

1.

2.

3.

4.

5.

As Tool 4 touched on, things that worked in the past don't always work in the present, and things that work in the present in the short-term don't always work in the long term. In attempt to increase your awareness, try to identify some of the consequences of your unsuccessful attempted solutions to stress in the past.

Example

Autopilot Coping Skill (from Tool 4)	Current or Past Negative Consequences
Smoke pot	Lost job
Careless sex	Guilt, awkward relationship, STD

Awareness of Consequences Log

Autopilot Coping Skill (from Tool 4)	Current or Past Negative Consequences

Some things I will try the next time I feel stressed are:

1.

2.

3.

4.

5.

6.

7.

8.

9.

10.

Challenging distorted thoughts doesn't always make them go away, but it can put up enough of a "fight" that feelings aren't quite so intense, and it may be at least slightly easier to use some of the skills you identified in Tool 6. Utilize the following *thought log* to attempt to *challenge* or generate some more *rational responses* to the distorted thoughts you identified in Tool 3. Remember, since stress often results from those "shoulds" that add pressure, responses should focus on ways of taking the pressure off.

Example

Distorted Thought	Rational Response
I must do well on this test.	I'd like to do well, but if I don't, it's not the end of the world—putting pressure on myself makes it less likely I'll succeed.
This is too much, I can't do it.	I've done similar things before—even though it feels hard, I've done many hard things in my life—I can get through this.
She's probably going to yell at me any second now.	She may not yell at me, and if she does, I've had people yell at me before—I don't have to like it, but I can cope with snappy people.

Thought Log

Distorted Thought	Rational Response

As a refresher, *core beliefs* are deeply engrained beliefs that serve as filters through which we process information. All of our distorted thinking is the product of one or more harmful beliefs. This technique asks us to take a thought and continue to ask, "What would that mean about us if it were true?" until we get at what the core belief is at the bottom of the distorted thought. If necessary, consult the section of this chapter about noting beliefs that often contribute to stress. Also, remember that many people need a therapist's help to assist with this for a period of time.

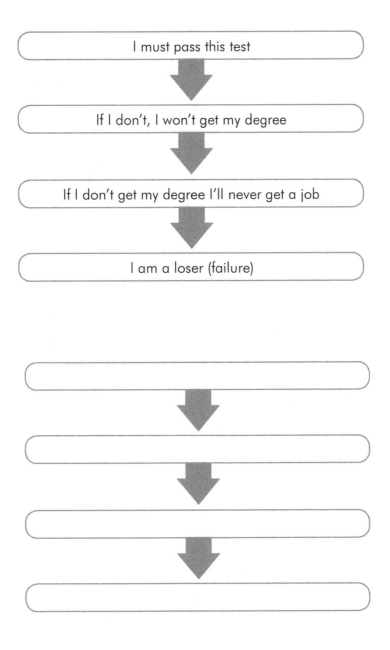

Remember, beliefs come in pairs. For each unhealthy belief you identified, formulate in your words what the exact opposite of that would mean to you. Flexible language remains important.

Example

My Beliefs

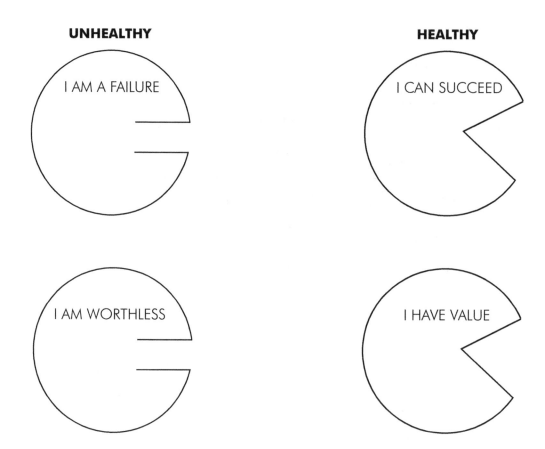

UNHEALTHY

I AM A FAILURE

I AM WORTHLESS

HEALTHY

I CAN SUCCEED

I HAVE VALUE

My Beliefs

UNHEALTHY   **HEALTHY**

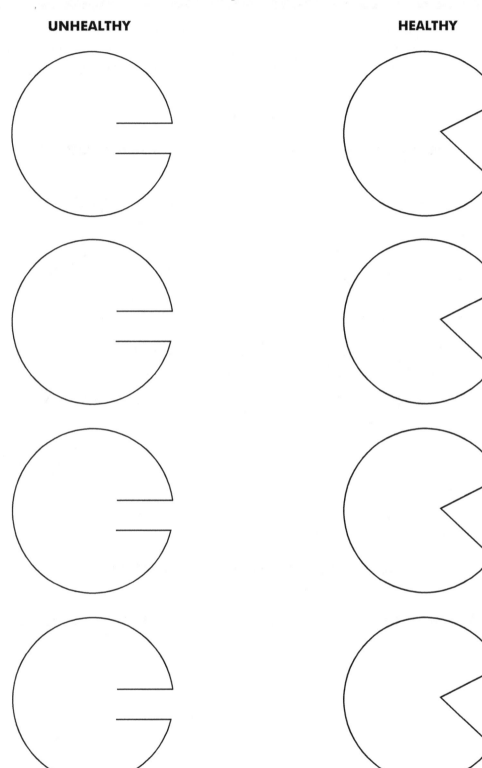

The strength of our beliefs significantly influence how often we feel stressful emotions and how strongly we experience them. Take a few minutes and try to assign a strength to each healthy and unhealthy belief. Usually, the easiest way is to use percentages so the total between the unhealthy belief and the healthy one equals 100 percent.

Example

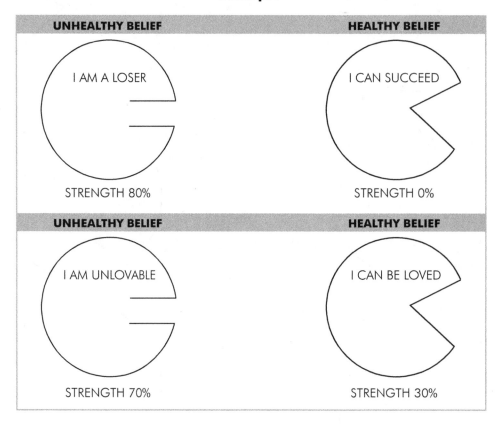

Rating the Strength of my Beliefs

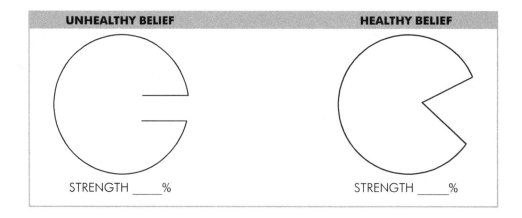

The following questions may be helpful in reflecting back on different periods of your life to uncover some of the experiences you counted as evidence to support your belief (legs to hold up your table). You may need assistance from your therapist to get the most out of this tool.

The first time I ever remember feeling _____[belief]

was _____

The people in my life who influenced me to feel that way were:

Family members _____
_____

Friends/Peers _____
_____

Other significant people _____
_____

Experiences during my elementary school years _____
_____
_____

Experiences during my junior high years _____
_____
_____

Experiences during my high school years _____
_____
_____

Experiences during my college/young adult years _____
_____
_____

Significant experiences since then _____
_____
_____

Use the exercise on the previous page to try to insert some of the "evidence" from your past that you have "counted" to support each belief.

Example

FAILURE

Cut from basketball — Leg 1
Ridiculed by teacher — Leg 2
Yelled at by father — Leg 3
Unfriended — Leg 4
Car accident — Leg 5

Evidence that I am a failure:

Leg 1: Cut from 8th grade basketball team

Leg 2: Ridiculed for science project by teacher

Leg 3: Father yelled at me in garage for mistake on construction project

Leg 4: Was unfriended by classmate

Leg 5: Got into a car accident while texting and driving

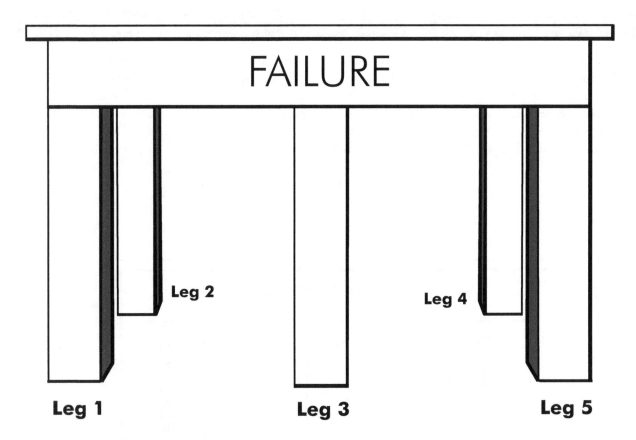

Evidence that I am a failure:

Leg 1:

Leg 2:

Leg 3:

Leg 4:

Leg 5:

Because of how our filters are set up, we often notice instances that support the unhealthy beliefs more than we notice those that may support our opposite, healthy beliefs. But almost always, that "evidence" exists as well. One valuable tool involves forcing ourselves to look back over those very same periods of life purposefully looking to see the evidence that supports our healthy beliefs. Many people rely on family members or friends who were around them during each period of life to help them "notice" such evidence. Even if they share things they see as "counting" that you don't think "should count" write them down anyway—a tool to help with that is provided later!

Example

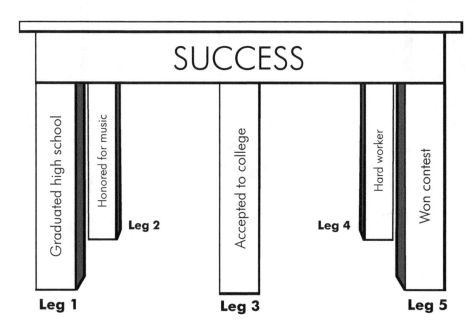

Evidence that I can succeed:

Leg 1: I graduated from high school.

Leg 2: I was honored on numerous occasions for my music.

Leg 3: I was accepted to college.

Leg 4: I am a hard worker and can accomplish much when I put my mind to it.

Leg 5: I won the contest last week.

Healthy Evidence Log

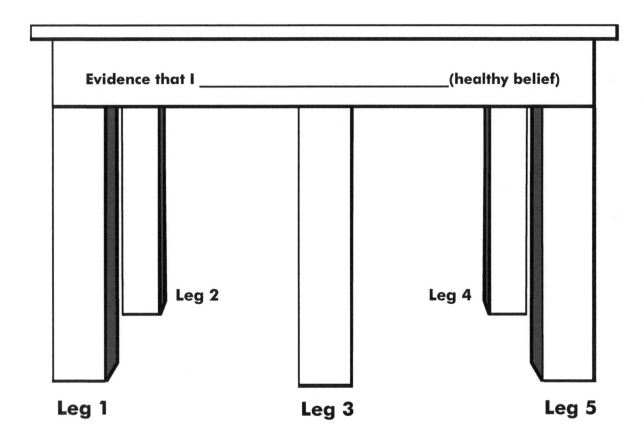

Evidence that I _____(healthy belief)

Leg 1

Leg 2

Leg 3

Leg 4

Leg 5

Leg 1:

Leg 2:

Leg 3:

Leg 4:

Leg 5:

Beliefs *mean* different things to different people. Refer to Tool 13 in Chapter 2 for examples of what it might mean to *have value*. Using that as a guide, compile a list of a few things that support your healthy beliefs about yourself.

Example

Belief
1. Can be liked

Components
1. Girls paying attention to me
2. Having friends
3. Popular in social group

Belief

1.

Components

1.

2.

3.

2.

1.

2.

3.

3.

1.

2.

3.

Purposefully pay attention to things in life that might count as evidence that your healthy belief could be true.

Example
Evidence log that I can be liked/loved

Date	Evidence
3/12	Mom hugged me
3/13	Aunt sent me care package
3/16	Friend called to check on me
3/20	Got invited to a party
3/22	Scout leader said he appreciated me

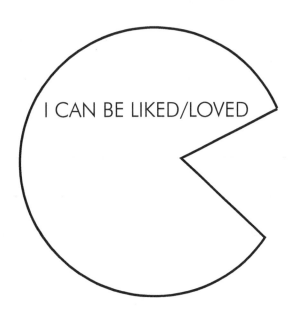

I CAN BE LIKED/LOVED

Evidence log that I can be liked/loved

Date	Evidence

Living a balanced lifestyle is important for recovery of any kind. In his book *The Road to Recovery*, Allan Gates (1995) stressed four areas of general well-being on which to focus to find balance in one's life. They are physical, emotional, relational, and spiritual. *Self-care* is a term used to describe how well we tend to these four important areas of life. If one or more of these areas is not sufficiently nurtured, we become unbalanced. The following life satisfaction scale can help you assess areas that may be important for you to address. This tool then focuses on physical well-being, with the following three tools addressing the emotional, relational, and spiritual areas.

Place a number from 0 to 10 on the line next to each item below, with 0 representing "worst I have ever been," and 10, "best I have ever been."

Marriage/Romantic relationship   ____

Mental/Emotional health   ____

Career/Employment   ____

Recreation/Hobbies   ____

Spiritual life   ____

Physical health   ____

Friendships/Social life   ____

Physical environment (home, cars, etc.)   ____

Church/Religious participation   ____

Extended family   ____

Relationship with children (list each separately)

_____   ____

_____   ____

_____   ____

_____   ____

Am I satisfied with my diet/eating habits? Am I taking vitamins? Eating regular meals? Overweight? Underweight? Drinking enough water? Binge eating? Purging? _____

_____

_____

Changes I may need to consider in this area may be

_____

_____

_____

Am I getting sufficient sleep? Do I have trouble falling asleep? Staying asleep? Am I doing things before I go to bed that are helping me? Hurting me? Taking medications properly? Bedtime routine? _____

_____

_____

Changes I may need to consider in this area may be_____

_____

_____

Am I satisfied with my physical exercise? _____

_____

What changes can I make in this area? _____

_____

Five changes I will make to improve my physical well-being are:

1.

2.

3.

4.

5.

TOOL 16 EMOTIONAL WELLNESS

What negative emotions will I most likely experience this week? _____

_____

_____

_____

Am I satisfied with how I deal with those emotions? _____

_____

_____

_____

What have I tried to manage my emotions that has *not* worked? _____

_____

_____

_____

What have I tried that has worked? _____

_____

_____

_____

Am I satisfied with how I spend my time? _____

_____

_____

_____

Am I doing my therapy homework? Am I journaling? _____

_____

_____

_____

_____

Am I satisfied with my hobbies/interests? _____

_____

_____

_____

Changes I may need to consider in this area are: _____

_____

_____

_____

Five changes I can make to improve my emotional well-being are:

1.

2.

3.

4.

5.

If conflict arises with another person this week, that person is likely to be

_____

_____

_____

The person I am in conflict with most often is

_____

_____

_____

The person in my life I have the most difficult time standing up to is

_____

_____

_____

The person in my life I sometimes treat poorly but wish I didn't is

_____

_____

_____

Am I generally satisfied with the relationships I have in my life? _____

_____

_____

_____

If I were to meet new friends who shared common interests and values, three places I could potentially meet them are

_____

_____

_____

One change I could make to improve a relationship today is

_____

_____

_____

Changes I may need to consider in this area are

_____

_____

_____

Five changes I could make to manage my relationships better are:

1.

2.

3.

4.

5.

To me, God is

_____

_____

_____

I incorporate my faith into my life in the following way(s) _____

_____

_____

_____

Spiritual practices, disciplines, and exercises in which I engage regularly are

_____

_____

_____

Questions I have about my faith are

_____

_____

_____

One reason I think I need to grow in my faith is

_____

_____

_____

One reason I have not made my faith a greater priority in my life is

_____

_____

_____

My faith can serve as a resource in my recovery in the following ways _____

_____

_____

_____

Five changes I could make to enhance my spiritual growth are:

1.

2.

3.

4.

5.

Proper "sleep hygiene" (attempts to influence sleep through change of habits and environment) and a healthy diet are cornerstones of healthy self-care. Many people believe that the only tool for combating sleep difficulties is medication. Sometimes pharmacologic interventions are necessary to address certain sleep-related concerns. However, sleep difficulties often respond to a variety of environmental interventions as well. Research has also confirmed that nutrition can play a vital role in a variety of areas related to recovery. Review the following sleep hygiene and healthy diet guidelines and consider changes you may like to make in these areas:

Sleep Hygiene

Do:
- Monitor room temperature
- Go to bed at the same time daily
- Get up at same time daily
- Use bed for only sleep and sex
- Keep bedroom quiet while sleeping
- Take sleeping meds *as prescribed*
- Establish bedtime routine
- Go to bed when you are tired

Don't:
- Use alcohol or drugs not prescribed for you by a doctor to sleep
- Eat heavily before bed
- Participate in overly stimulating activity before bed
- Drink caffeine/eat sugars cloes to bedtime
- Watch graphic movies or morbid TV shows close to bedtime
- Take another person's sleeping pills
- Lie in bed for hours if you can't sleep

Healthy Eating

Healthy eating is:
- Eating what you enjoy
- Eating when you are hungry
- Eating that which sustains you
- Eating reasonable portions
- Eating regularly

Unhealthy eating is:
- Skipping meals
- Binge eating
- Eating only sweets
- Overeating when angry/hurt
- Eating too much
- Eating too little

Results of unhealthy eating:
- Obesity
- Type 2 diabetes
- Anorexia
- Bulimia
- Anemia
- Social isolation
- Low self-esteem
- Self-hatred

Distorted Thoughts About Food

- "I live to eat."
- "I have to have this food now."
- "Food is bad for me."
- "If I eat, I am a bad person."
- "Food means being out of control."
- "Food is necessary for socialization."
- "Food is necessary for celebration."
- "Eating is wrong."
- "Eating protects me/helps me feel secure."
- "Food equals weakness."
- "If I don't look like _____, I am a failure/undesirable."

Five changes related to sleeping/eating I can make are:

1.

2.

3.

4.

5.

Now, to help you with those "heat of the moment" reactions, refer to Tool 20 in Chapter 2 to develop your cards. Remember, the coping card gives you alternative things to *do* "in the moment." Cue cards help you with how to *think*.

Examples

Coping Card

When I'm tempted to _____Drink_____ **(behavior from Tool 4),**

I can (choices from Tool 6):

1. _Go for a run._

2. _Do my breathing exercises._

3. _Use progressive muscle relaxation._

Your Coping Card

When I'm tempted to _____ **(behavior from Tool 4),**

I can (choices from Tool 6):

1. _____

2. _____

3. _____

Cognitive Cue Card

Just because <u>somebody expects something of me</u> (trigger)

doesn't mean <u>I'm obligated to do it.</u> (stressful response).

Your Cognitive Cue Card

Just because _____ (trigger)

doesn't mean _____ (stressful response).

Chapter 4 **Toxic Relationships**

COMMON BELIEFS

- I am undeserving.
- I am defective.
- I am vulnerable.
- I am unlovable.
- I am dependent.
- I will undergo subjugation.
- I will be abandoned ("I can't be OK alone, others will leave me.")

I AM DEFECTIVE   I AM VULNERABLE   I AM UNLOVABLE

COMMON DISTORTIONS

- Should statements (self and others)
- Mind reading
- Personalization
- Discounting the positive

COMMON AUTOMATIC THOUGHTS

- "He should know what I need, I shouldn't have to tell him!"
- "If I stand up for myself, I might get left."
- "If I disagree, she may not love me anymore."
- "I guess I have to put up with this, because I couldn't get any better anyway."
- "He should do what I want as soon as I say to."
- "It is unacceptable if he doesn't approve of me."
- "He has to see things the way I do!"

COMMON FEELINGS

- Guilt
- Shame
- Anger
- Resentment
- Being trapped
- Helplessness
- Hopelessness
- Hurt
- Rejection

COMMON BEHAVIORS

- Threatening
- Cowering
- Staying in bad relationships
- Leaving but coming back

Triggers in this area are much different than the triggers we have examined previously for low self-esteem or stress and those we look at later for emotions such as depression, anxiety, or anger. Triggers for toxic relationships are more specific and obviously have to involve another person. We call these relational triggers. *Relational triggers* can be certain people, words said, or actions taken or not taken. Take a few minutes to answer the following questions that may increase your awareness of your toxic relationship triggers.

To me, signs of a toxic relationship are_____

I know I am/wonder if I am in one because _____

I seem to feel the worst about myself when I am around the following person/people

_____

Common characteristics in people around whom I feel bad include _____

_____

The most hurtful or upsetting things people say to me have to do with what subject/issue

_____

My toxic relationship triggers are:

1.

2.

3.

4.

5.

Feelings produced in toxic relationships can run the gamut. Some people often feel sad or hurt, while others live in constant fear. *Refer to your face sheet* (Tool 2 in Chapter 2) to identify what feelings you frequently experience or have experienced while in toxic relationships.

My feelings in toxic relationships are:

1.

2.

3.

4.

5.

The following questions are designed to help you identify distorted thoughts specifically related to toxic relationships. Relationship-related thoughts can take many forms and include any of the 10 distortions.

When _____ (trigger; see Tool 1 in this chapter) **happens,**

and I feel _____ (feelings; see Tool 2 in this chapter),

what am I usually telling myself?

If I were in a cartoon, what would the bubble above my head be saying?

If there were a tape recorder in my head recording my every thought, what would it be saying when someone pushed "play?"

Example

I felt ...	...because I thought...
Betrayed	He shouldn't lie to me—I thought I could trust him.
Rejected	He left me for another woman—I must not be pretty enough.
Intimidated	If I voice my opinion, I might get hurt. I'd better keep my mouth shut.

Thoughts/Feelings Awareness Log

I felt ...	...because I thought...

"Autopilot" unhealthy coping skills used to cope with relational stress can vary drastically. Some people nag, attack, and demean. Others avoid the other person completely. Some turn to outside unhealthy behaviors. Spend a few minutes trying to identify unhealthy behavior habits you may have developed in response to these feelings.

The last time I felt my low self-esteem, I _____.

Other things I have done in the past in an attempt to cope that have in some way hurt me are:

Some of my "go to"/"autopilot" coping skills are:

1.

2.

3.

4.

5.

As Tool 4 touched on, things that worked in the past don't always work in the present, and things that work in the present in the short term don't always work in the long term. To increase your awareness, try to identify some of the consequences of unsuccessful solutions you used to address to relational difficulties in the past.

Example

Autopilot Coping Skill (from Tool 4)	Current or Past Negative Consequences
Shut down, never stood up for self	Depression, anxiety, self-esteem got worse for 10 years
Yelled back and threw something at him	He broke my arm I am not allowed at my daughter's birthday parties

Awareness of Consequences Log

Autopilot Coping Skill (from Tool 4)	Current or Past Negative Consequences

Some things I will try the next time I experience a relational trigger are:

1.

2.

3.

4.

5.

Challenging distorted thoughts doesn't always make them go away, but it can put up enough of a "fight" so that feelings aren't quite so intense and it may be slightly easier to use some of the skills you identified in Tool 6. Utilize the following *thought log* to attempt to *challenge* or generate some more *rational responses* to the distorted thoughts you identified in Tool 3.

Example

Distorted Thought	Rational Response
"He shouldn't lie to me—I thought I could trust him."	"He has lied to me consistently for 6 years—as hard as it is to admit this, there is an obvious pattern. He is likely to continue to do it. I just have to decide if he'll be doing it to me or not."
"He left me for another woman—I must not be pretty enough."	"He has left 8 women. It doesn't mean I'm not pretty—it means he is unfaithful. He left multiple women, some of whom were attractive and some of whom weren't—this is not about me."
"If I voice my opinion, I might get hurt. I'd better keep my mouth shut."	"If I don't do something, I'll stay miserable. Intimidation is what he has done to keep me quiet. I have support. I need to focus on keeping my daughter and me safe and facing my fears."

Thought Log

Distorted Thought	Rational Response

As a refresher, *core beliefs* are deeply engrained beliefs that serve as filters through which we process information. All of our distorted thinking is the product of one or more harmful beliefs. This technique asks us to take a thought and continue to ask, "What would that mean if it were true?" until we get at what the core belief is at the bottom of the distorted thought. If necessary, refer back to earlier in the chapter where we noted beliefs that often contribute to stress. Also, remember many people need a therapist's help with this for a period of time.

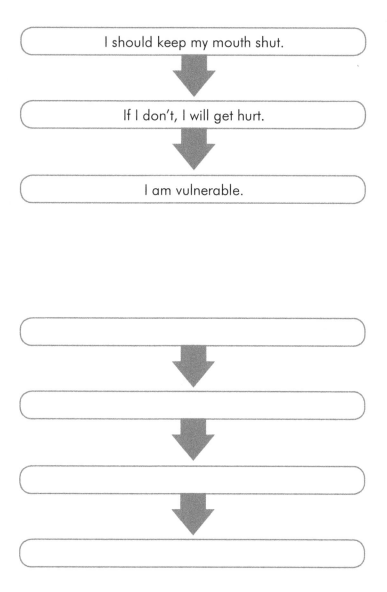

I should keep my mouth shut.

If I don't, I will get hurt.

I am vulnerable.

Remember, beliefs come in pairs. For each unhealthy belief you identified, formulate in your words what the exact opposite of that would mean to you. Flexible language remains important.

Example

My Beliefs

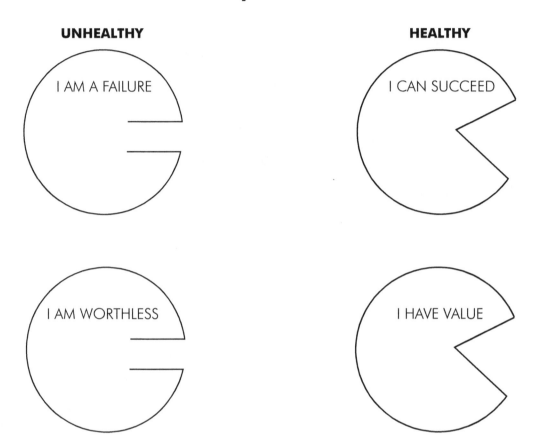

UNHEALTHY   **HEALTHY**

I AM A FAILURE   I CAN SUCCEED

I AM WORTHLESS   I HAVE VALUE

My Beliefs

UNHEALTHY　　　　　　　　　　　　**HEALTHY**

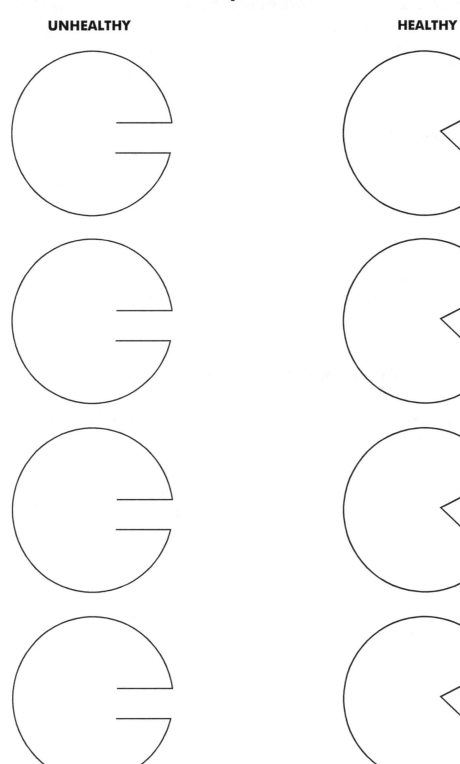

The strength of our beliefs significantly influences how often we feel stressful emotions and how strongly we experience them. Take a few minutes and try to assign a strength to each healthy and unhealthy belief. Usually, the easiest way is to use percentages so the total for unhealthy and healthy beliefs equals 100 percent.

Example

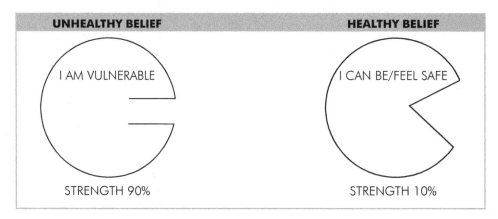

Rating the Strength of My Beliefs

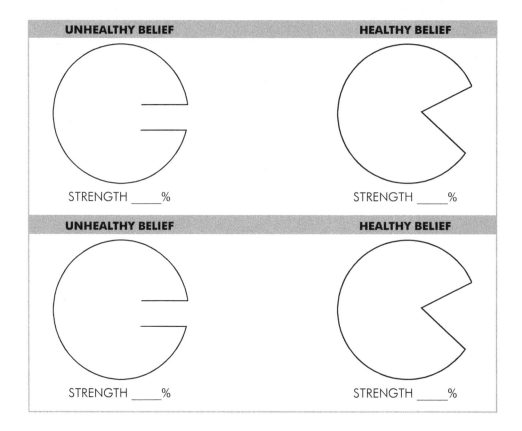

The following questions may be helpful in reflecting back on different periods of your life to uncover some of the experiences you counted as evidence to support your belief (legs to hold up your table). You may need assistance from your therapist to get the most out of this tool.

The first time I ever remember feeling _____[belief]

was _____

The people in my life who influenced me to feel that way were:

Family members _____

_____

Friends/Peers _____

_____

Other significant people _____

_____

Experiences during my elementary school years _____

_____

_____

Experiences during my junior high years _____

_____

_____

Experiences during my high school years _____

_____

_____

Experiences during my college/young adult years _____

_____

_____

Significant experiences since then _____

_____

_____

Use the exercise the previous page to try to insert some of the "evidence" from your past that you have "counted" to support each belief.

Example

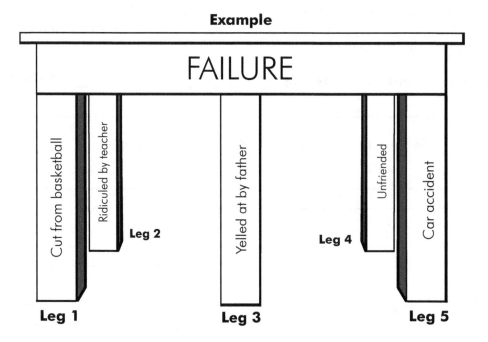

FAILURE

Cut from basketball — Leg 1

Ridiculed by teacher — Leg 2

Yelled at by father — Leg 3

Unfriended — Leg 4

Car accident — Leg 5

Evidence that I am a failure:

Leg 1: Cut from 8th grade basketball team

Leg 2: Ridiculed for science project by teacher

Leg 3: Father yelled at me in garage for mistake on construction project

Leg 4: Was unfriended by classmate

Leg 5: Got into car accident while texting and driving

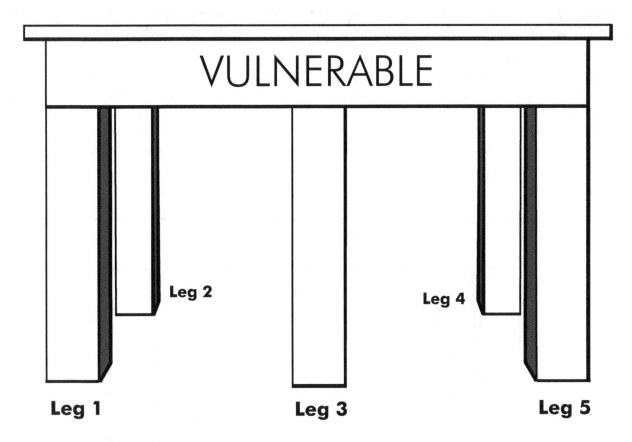

VULNERABLE

Leg 1

Leg 2

Leg 3

Leg 4

Leg 5

Evidence that I was vulnerable:

Leg 1:

Leg 2:

Leg 3:

Leg 4:

Leg 5:

Because of how our filters are set up, we often notice instances that support the unhealthy beliefs more than we notice experiences that may support our opposite, healthy beliefs, but almost always, that "evidence" exists as well. One valuable tool involves forcing ourselves to look back over those very same periods of life purposefully looking to see the evidence that supports our healthy beliefs. Many people rely on family members or friends who were around them during each period of life to help them "notice" such evidence. Even if they share things they see as "counting" that you don't think "should count" write them down anyway—a tool to help with that is provided later!

Example

Evidence that I can be safe:

Leg 1: My uncle protected me even though my parents did not.

Leg 2: I felt secure at Grammy's house.

Leg 3: I felt safe at my youth pastor's house.

Leg 4: Nobody hurt me once I moved to the Thomas House.

Leg 5: I felt safe in my therapist's waiting room.

Healthy Evidence Log

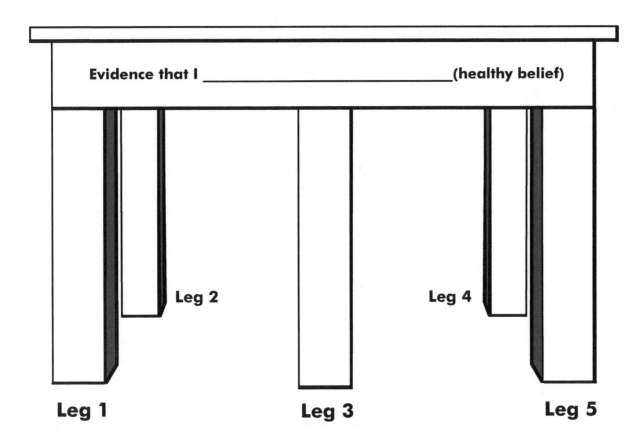

Evidence that I _____(healthy belief)

Leg 1

Leg 2

Leg 3

Leg 4

Leg 5

Leg 1:

Leg 2:

Leg 3:

Leg 4:

Leg 5:

Beliefs *mean* different things to different people. Refer to Tool 13 in Chapter 2 for examples of what it might mean to *have value*. Using that as a guide, compile a list of a few things that support your healthy beliefs about yourself.

Example

Belief	**Components**
1. I can be safe/fell secure	**1.** Safe people
	2. Safe places
	3. Safe moments

Belief	**Components**
1.	**1.**
	2.
	3.

2.	**1.**
	2.
	3.

3.	**1.**
	2.
	3.

Purposefully pay attention to things in life that might count as evidence that your healthy belief could be true.

Example

Evidence that I can be safe/feel secure

Date	Evidence
9/12	Drove home with no accident
9/13	Hug from John
9/16	Comforted by aunt
9/20	Hung out with men all evening and felt secure
9/22	People at social gathering seemed less threatening

I CAN FEEL SAFE/SECURE

Evidence that I can be _____ (healthy statement) log

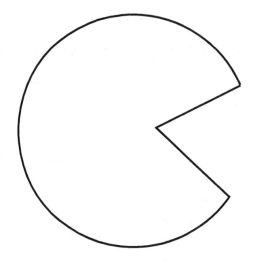

Date	Evidence

Healthy relationships are an important part of recovery. Some people *desperately* feel that they need relationships. Thus, at different stages of their lives, they may attempt to develop relationships very quickly and tend to foster intimacy and trust in relationships sooner than is wise considering how little they really know the person. Some people get hurt in relationships and eventually have been hurt so many times that trusting again is difficult. Therefore, some people put up "walls" that keep people from getting in. These walls work in the sense that they keep people from getting close to hurt them. However, they keep people from getting in to help them as well. Others never put up these walls and continue to seek relationships but do so in unhelpful ways and with unhealthy people. Relationships are important to everybody. The reality is that people need people, and the quality of the people we have in our lives can make or break our ability to live fulfilling lives.

Take a few minutes to examine the relationships you have, writing them in the circles in the diagram that follows. Use each ring of the circles to show how close you consider each person to be. People in your innermost circle are people you would share anything with, no matter how personal. People in your outermost circle are those who are in your life in some capacity (whether you like it or not) but that you would not trust with any of your personal information.

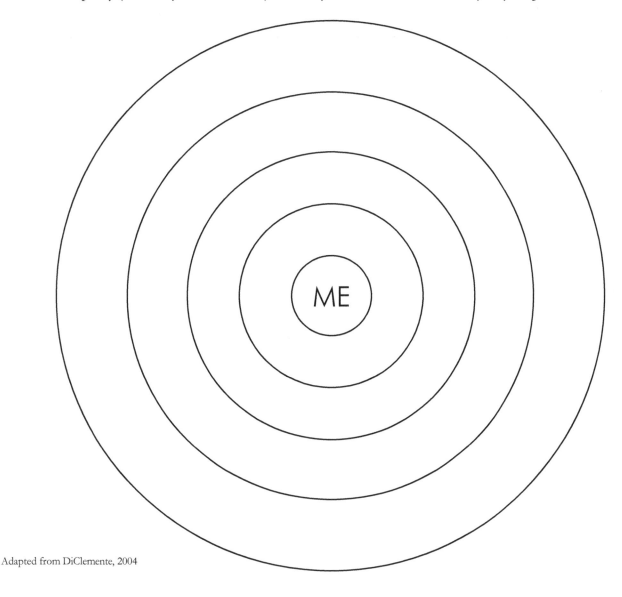

Adapted from DiClemente, 2004

Examining your "circles," consider whom you might like to include on your support team.

My Support Team

Name   **Phone Number**

1._____   _____

2._____   _____

3._____   _____

4._____   _____

5._____   _____

When examining their relationship circles, different people note different patterns. The reality is that there are several different types of "unhealthy circles." People who put walls up often have no (or few) people in the inner circles but have multiple people in the outer circles. Others may have one extremely important person in circle one but few, if any, other people in their lives. Still others enter several names into their circles but observe that they are all unhealthy in one way or another. A final common theme involves people looking at their circles and recognizing that they have very few relationships. Period. If you are in the latter camp, your initial task is simply meeting new people.

Would you like to add to your circles people who currently aren't there?

_____

_____

What would be some of the pros of having additional people in my life?

_____

_____

What would be some of the cons?

_____

_____

Some people participate in this exercise and think, "Oh my gosh—I've got to add people to my circles" and simply go out and strike up relationships with the first people that come along. This obviously poses a separate set of problems that would cause one of the other types of unhealthy circles. So, having people in our lives is important but so is discernment: being able to recognize who is safe and who is not, who is healthy and who is not. In their book *Safe People*, Henry Cloud and John Townsend outline some characteristics of safe people that may be helpful to consider.

Safe People:

Meeting New People

Some qualities of people I'd like in my circle include _____

_____

_____

_____

Some things I enjoy doing that I could have as potential common interests with new acquaintances or friends are _____

_____

_____

_____

Places I could possibly meet people with these qualities/interests include _____

_____

_____

_____

One small step I am willing to take this week to further my potential support team is

_____

_____

_____

Asking for help appropriately can be a challenge for many people. Many families (often unknowingly) send its members the message, "It's weak to ask for help." People who have heard this message repeatedly as children may still believe as adults the myth that "asking for help means I am incompetent" or "it means I am giving someone the upper hand" or "it means I'll be taken advantage of." Thus, one of the most common unhealthy behaviors exhibited in toxic relationships is the inability to ask for help. Many predators or other controlling people can detect that quality quickly in people and may choose them for relationships for that very reason! They know such people are easily isolated and taken advantage of. Tool 17 is designed to help you begin to think about making progress in this area.

With which of the following can you relate?

- "Asking for help means I am weak."
- "No one will like me if they really get to know me."
- "If I ask for help, I will get hurt."
- "If I ask for help, I will get rejected/turned down."
- "If I ask, people are obligated to help me."
- "If they can't meet my needs, they deserve to be punished/are not worth having in my life at all."

In my family, asking for help was

_____

_____

_____

The last time I asked for help was

_____

_____

_____

Their response was

_____

_____

_____

When I ask for help, I feel

_____

_____

_____

Characteristics of people I may want to ask for help are

_____

_____

_____

Qualities of unsafe people I do not want to have to depend on are

_____

_____

_____

People in my circles I am already comfortable asking for help are:

1.

2.

3.

People in my circles I am not comfortable asking for help yet but could be in the future are:

1.

2.

3.

People in my circles I am not comfortable asking for help in a personal area but may consider asking for something small include:

1.

2.

3.

One small step I am willing to take in this area is:

A boundary is a line of demarcation that separates one entity from another. It defines where one thing ends and another begins (Cloud & Townsend, 2002). Boundaries can be geographical, professional, emotional, sexual, spiritual, or physical to name just a few. In terms of relationships, boundaries describe limits that people set with one another. The boundaries we set with others determine how close in we allow people in our circles. They determine how close we are emotionally to others. They influence how we allow people to treat us and thereby what we experience in our relationships.

Many people grew up in chaotic families where boundaries were not respected or modeled. If you grew up in such a family, you may have a difficult time setting boundaries with yourself or others, enabling you to feel safe in relationships and to not be taken advantage of. You also may struggle to not violate others' boundaries.

Developing and maintaining healthy boundaries is essential for living a healthy and balanced life. Healthy boundaries will not only help you feel more safe and secure in the relationships you are in, it will also help the other people you care about feel more secure and less threatened in the relationship as well. Following are a few principles regarding boundaries that may assist you with learning how to use this tool.

Healthy Boundaries

People who have healthy boundaries
- Interact with people effectively
- Frequently get what they want in relationships
- Know what they will and will not do
- Know what they will and will not allow others to do
- Can set limits and still love
- Do not violate the personal space of others
- Do not take on responsibilities of others
- Can be responsible *to* others without feeling responsible *for* them
- Feel safe and secure
- Have healthy "circles"

People who have unhealthy boundaries
- Frequently have difficulty in relationships
- Have difficulty getting their needs met in relationships
- Trust too easily and share too much personal information with the wrong people
- Trust too little and don't have people that they can open up to
- Violate the personal space of others
- Ask inappropriately personal questions of people they don't know well
- Feel responsible for other people's behavior and feelings
- Often live lives driven by guilt
- Choose actions based on what will please others rather than their convictions
- Tolerate unhealthy or inappropriate behaviors from others
- Feel unsafe in relationships
- Have unhealthy "circles"

Failing to set boundaries in past relationships has hurt me in the following ways

_____

_____

_____

My biggest fear with setting boundaries is _____

_____

_____

_____

After I set a boundary, I usually feel _____

_____

_____

_____

People in my circles who I currently have boundary difficulties with are

_____

_____

_____

One boundary I will set this week is

_____

_____

_____

Your last tool involved setting boundaries. While this can take many forms, the most common method of boundary setting simply involves *saying no*. While this sounds like a simple concept and everyone who can talk is capable of saying no, saying it to people we need to at certain times can present a major challenge. Have you ever kicked yourself by thinking something like, "Why in the world did I say yes to that?" Some people routinely say yes when they mean no. If you are in this category, you may find it helpful to return to Tool 8 to gain some insight into why you struggle with this. The following questions may provide you with a refresher:

- If I tell him or her no, what am I afraid might happen?
- What might he or she do?
- What would that mean about me?
- How could I cope with that?

Do these questions bring you any insights? What themes did you identify?

Many core beliefs can prevent us from saying no when a big part of us wants to. Frequently, we find themes related to abandonment or approval seeking to be involved. If this was the case for you, you may want to review evidence logs documenting evidence that you are likable, whether people like you or not, and evidence regarding the stability of your relationship with that person.

The person in my circles I can say no to most easily is _____.

The person in my circle I find it the most difficult to say no to is _____.

What characteristics seem to make it easier or harder for me to say no to people?

_____

_____

_____

One small step I will take to say no to someone this week is

_____

_____

_____

Coping Cards

The next time I am in a bad situation in a relationship, instead of

(unhealthy coping skill, Tool 4): _allowing myself to continue to get_
taken advantage of

I can:

1. _stand up for myself_

2. _talk to a counselor, pastor or family member_

3. _Leave for a weekend to give it some space to think_
objectively about my future

The next time I am in a bad situation in a relationship, instead of

(unhealthy coping skill, Tool 4):

I can:

1.

2.

3.

Cognitive Cue Card

Just because _I have been run over in_ _____ **doesn't mean** _I'm worthless. I know I have_
relationships

value because I'm talented, people care about me, and I go out of my way to help others

---

Cognitive Cue Card

Just because_____(unhelathy coping skill from tool 4),

doesn't mean _____(unhealthy belief),

I know_____(healthy belief), **is true because**_____

_____

Chapter 5 **Communication Skills**

COMMON BELIEFS

- Undeserving
- Unlovable
- Entitled
- Dependent
- Vulnerable
- Will be abandoned
- Will experience subjugation
- Will experience punishment

ENTITLED UNDESERVING DEPENDENT

COMMON DISTORTIONS

- Should statements (self and others)
- Mind reading
- Personalizing
- Discounting the positive
- Rationalization

COMMON AUTOMATIC THOUGHTS

- "I don't have a right to stand up for myself."
- "If they don't give me what I ask for, I will take it."
- "I always have to be right."
- "I deserve it; therefore, I will do whatever it takes to get it."
- "If I speak up I might get hurt."
- "If I assert myself, he/she might leave."
- "It's OK to yell because she didn't do what I asked."

COMMON FEELINGS

- Anger
- Fear
- Intimidation
- Sadness
- Rejection
- Hurt
- Helplessness

COMMON BEHAVIORS

- Attacking
- Yelling
- Put downs
- Passive aggression
- Shutting down
- Avoidance

TOOL 1 IDENTIFICATION OF TRIGGERS

Similar to with toxic relationships, triggers for communication skills are usually relational triggers. However, toxic relationships are, by their nature, unhealthy in some way, whereas effective communication skills are necessary to maintain healthy relationships and often to function in daily life and achieve everyday goals. When we need something, are trying to problem-solve with others, have a request, or are being pressured to do things we don't want to do are common situations in which people have difficulty communicating effectively. Take a few minutes to answer the following questions that may increase your awareness of your triggers related to communication skills.

To me, communication is

_____

_____

To me, the phrase "You cannot not communicate" means _____

_____

_____

For me, the biggest obstacle to effective communication is

_____

_____

The person/people I have the most difficult time communicating with is/are

_____

It's probably harder with this person/people because

_____

_____

My triggers for communication problems are:

1.

2.

3.

4.

5.

A later tool is provided to assist you in communicating feelings to others in a helpful way. The obvious step that precedes communication of feelings is awareness of feelings. Some people don't even know how they feel, let alone how to express those feelings. There are no feelings specifically experienced more than others in relation to communication skills. Feelings can run the gamut. Refer to your *face sheet* (Tool 2 in Chapter 2) to identify what feelings you frequently experience related to communication skills.

My communication-related feelings are:

1.

2.

3.

4.

5.

TOOL 3 IDENTIFICATION OF DISTORTED THOUGHTS

The following questions are designed to help you identify your distorted thoughts specifically related to communication problems.

The following questions are designed to help you identify your distorted thoughts specifically related to low self-esteem:

When _____(trigger; see Tool 1 in this chapter) **happens,**

and I feel _____(feelings; see Tool 2 in this chapter),

what am I usually telling myself?

If I were in a cartoon, what would the bubble above my head be saying?

If there were a tape recorder in my head recording my every thought, what would it be saying when someone pushed "play?"

Example

I felt ...	...because I thought...
Hurt	She doesn't care about me.
Angry	He should give me what I asked for. I'll show him who's the boss.
Timid	I don't deserve to stand up for myself.

Thoughts/Feelings Awareness Log

I felt ...	...because I thought...

TOOL 4 GENERATE LIST OF UNHEALTHY "GO-TO" COPING SKILLS

"Autopilot" unhealthy coping skills frequently used to cope with communication problems are often relational in nature. Common examples include yelling, screaming, swearing, making demands, threatening, lying, and shutting down. Spend a few minutes trying to identify unhealthy behavior habits you may have developed in response to communication difficulties.

The last time I had a problem communicating, I _____

Other things I have done in the past in an attempt to get through to other people include _____

_____

_____

_____

_____

Some of my "go-to"/"autopilot" communication coping skills are:

1.

2.

3.

4.

5.

As Tool 4 touched on, things that worked in the past don't always work in the present, and things that work in the present in the short term don't always work in the long term. In attempt to increase your awareness, try to identify some of the consequences of your unsuccessful attempts to communicate when you were upset in the past.

Example

Autopilot Coping Skill (from Tool 4)	Current or Past Negative Consequences
Yell, swear	Hurt friend's feelings. She spends less time with me, I am lonely, have less support.
Shut down.	Boyfriend didn't know I was upset, tension in relationship, increased anxiety.

Awareness of Consequences Log

Autopilot Coping Skill (from Tool 4)	Current or Past Negative Consequences

Some things I will try the next time I communicate with someone are:

1.

2.

3.

4.

5.

Challenging distorted thoughts doesn't always make them go away, but it can put up enough of a "fight" that the feelings aren't quite so intense and thus it may be at least slightly easier to use some of the skills you identified in Tool 6. Utilize the following *thought log* to attempt to *challenge* or generate some more *rational responses* to the distorted thoughts you identified in Tool 3.

Example

Distorted Thought	Rational Response
She doesn't care about me.	Maybe she cares but just forgot. I have forgotten birthdays of people that I care about.
He should give me what I asked for. I'll show him who's the boss!	I think he should, but he isn't and he doesn't have to. My getting angry is only making things worse. The more I threaten, the less likely I will be to get what I want.
I don't deserve to stand up for myself.	I have as much right to stand up for myself as anyone else. If I don't stand up for myself, my daughter gets hurt also, and she definitely doesn't deserve it.

Thought Log

Distorted Thought	Rational Response

As a refresher, *core beliefs* are deeply engrained beliefs that serve as filters through which we process information. All of our distorted thinking is the product of one or more such beliefs. This technique asks us to keep asking ourselves, "What would that mean if it were true?" until we get at what the core belief is at the bottom of the distorted thought. If necessary, consult earlier parts of the chapter to note beliefs that often contribute to stress. Also, remember that many people need a therapist's help to assist with this for a period of time.

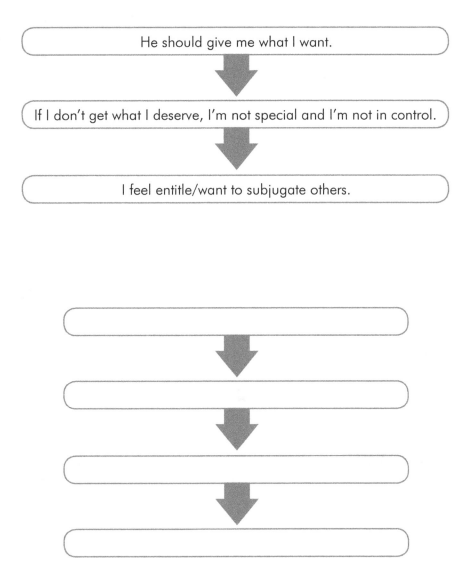

He should give me what I want.

If I don't get what I deserve, I'm not special and I'm not in control.

I feel entitle/want to subjugate others.

Remember, beliefs come in pairs. For each unhealthy belief you identified, formulate in your own words what the exact opposite of that would mean to you. Flexible language remains important.

Example

My Beliefs

UNHEALTHY

Entitlement
("I am special.")

HEALTHY

"I am just as deserving as anyone else."

Subjugation
("I must be in control.")

"It is OK to be out of control at times."

My Beliefs

UNHEALTHY

HEALTHY

The strength of our beliefs significantly influences how often we feel stressful emotions and how strongly we experience them. Take a few minutes and try to assign a strength to each healthy and unhealthy belief. Usually, the easiest way is to use percentages so the total of the strengths of the unhealthy and healthy beliefs equals 100 percent.

Example

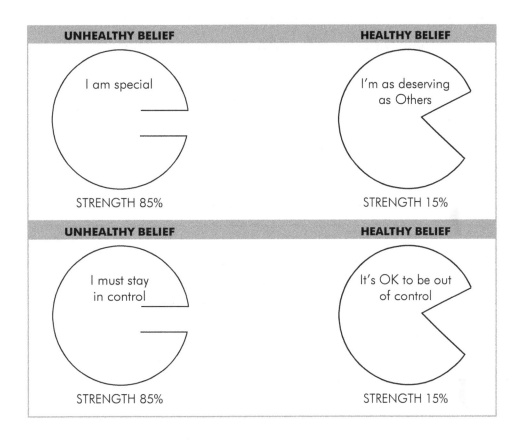

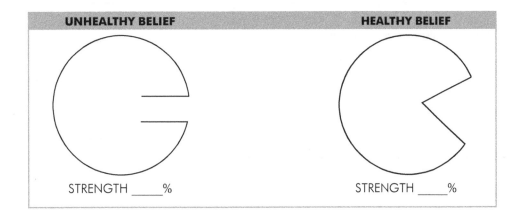

The following questions may be helpful in reflecting back on different periods of life to uncover some of the experiences you counted as evidence to support your belief (legs to hold up your table). You may need assistance from your therapist to get the most out of this tool.

The first time I ever remember feeling _____**[belief]**

was _____

The people in my life who influenced me to feel that way were:

Family members _____

_____

Friends/Peers _____

_____

Other significant people _____

_____

Experiences during my elementary school years _____

_____

_____

Experiences during my junior high years _____

_____

_____

Experiences during my high school years _____

_____

_____

Experiences during my college/young adult years _____

_____

_____

Significant experiences since then _____

_____

_____

Use the exercise on the left to try to insert some of the "evidence" from your past that you have "counted" to support each belief:

Example

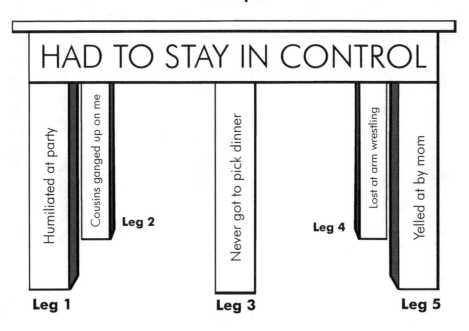

Evidence that I had to stay in control:

Leg 1: Friends at slumber party put my hand in warm water, and I wet my pants. All my friends made fun of me (for being out of control), and I was humiliated.

Leg 2: Cousins would gang up on me, hold me down, and tap my chest till I went crazy.

Leg 3: I never got a choice where we got to go eat—my older siblings always chose.

Leg 4: Every time I lost at arm wrestling I had to do my siblings' chores.

Leg 5: Every time I couldn't convince my mom to not go to her boyfriend's, I got yelled at.

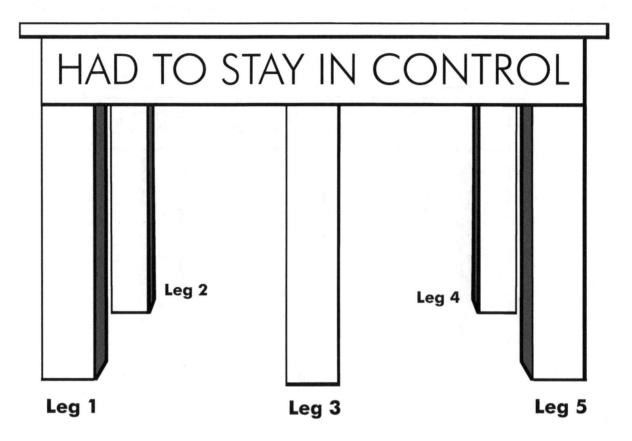

HAD TO STAY IN CONTROL

Leg 2

Leg 4

Leg 1

Leg 3

Leg 5

Evidence that I had to stay in control:

Leg 1:

Leg 2:

Leg 3:

Leg 4:

Leg 5:

Because of how our filters are set up, we often notice instances that support the unhealthy beliefs more than we notice experiences that may support our opposite, healthy beliefs. But almost always, that "evidence" exists as well. One valuable tool involves forcing ourselves to look back over those very same periods of life purposefully looking to see the evidence that supports our healthy beliefs. Many people ask family members or friends who were around them during each period of life to help them "notice" such evidence. Even if they share things they see as "counting" that you don't think "should count," write them down anyway— a tool is provided later to help with that!

Example

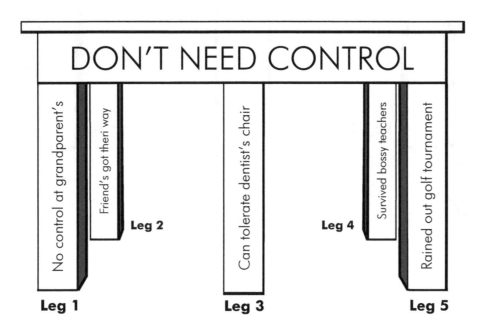

Evidence that I didn't have to be in control to be OK:

Leg 1: I was never in control at my grandparents' house, but I always had fun there.

Leg 2: Some of my friends always wanted things their way but treated me well.

Leg 3: I got to where I could tolerate sitting in the dentist's chair.

Leg 4: I survived bossy teachers.

Leg 5: One of my golf tournaments was rained out, but we had fun at the mall instead.

Healthy Evidence Log

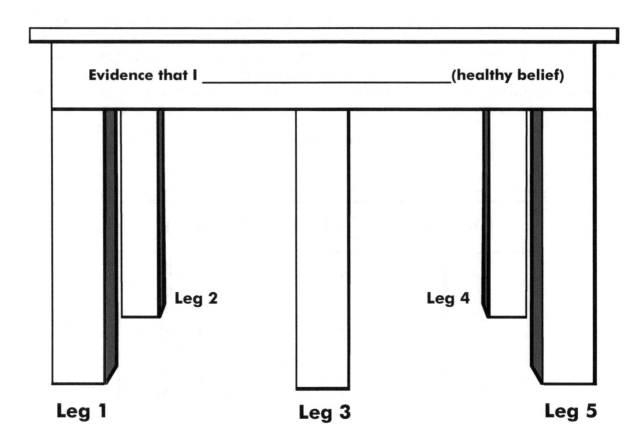

Evidence that I _____(healthy belief)

Leg 2

Leg 4

Leg 1   **Leg 3**   **Leg 5**

Leg 1:

Leg 2:

Leg 3:

Leg 4:

Leg 5:

TOOL 13 IDENTIFICATION OF COMPONENTS OF BELIEFS

Beliefs *mean* different things to different people. Refer to Tool 13 in Chapter 2 for examples of what it might mean to *have value*. Using that as a guide, compile a list of a few things that support your healthy beliefs about yourself.

Example

Belief

1. Can be out of control and OK

Components

1. Don't have to "win" conversations

2. Can defer to others' wishes

3. Other "out of control experiences

Belief

1.

Components

1.

2.

3.

2.

1.

2.

3.

3.

1.

2.

3.

Purposefully pay attention to things in life that might count as evidence that your healthy belief could be true.

Example

Evidence that I can be out of control and be OK

Date	Evidence
11/7	Let friend drive
11/9	Let wife have remote control all evening
11/10	Listened to daughter's music in the car
11/12	"Agreed to disagree" when my coworker was wrong
11/13	Let my wife initiate and control sex

I CAN BE OUT OF CONTROL AND BE OK

Evidence that I can be _____ (healthy belief) log

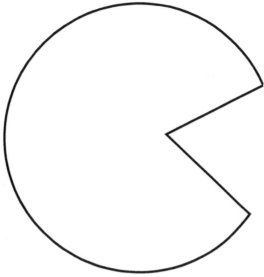

Date	Evidence

Effective communication involves two parts: the sending of the message and the receiving of the message. Communication can break down when messages are sent in unhelpful ways or received in unhelpful ways. To this point, we have been dealing mainly with your filters and how you receive messages. Effective communication also involves sending the message in a way that the other person can receive it in the spirit in which it was intended. Everyone has a more difficult time communicating effectively when one's emotions are running high. Some people are more prone to shut down and avoid, and others more prone to lash out. Developing an assertive communication style is an important skill for people seeking recovery of any kind.

What does it mean to you to be passive?_____

How about aggressive?_____

Passive-aggressive?_____

Meet
AGNES AGGRESSIVE

I'm loud, bossy and pushy.
I'm dominate and intimidate people.
I violate other's rights.
I "get my way" at anyone's expense.
I "step" on people.
I react instantly.

Meet
ALICE ASSERTIVE

I'm firm, direct and honest.
I respect the rights of others and recognize the importance of having my needs and right respected. I speak clearly and to the point. I'm confident about who I am. I realize I have choices about my life.

Meet
PATSY PASSIVE

I'm unable to speak up for my rights.
(I don't even know what my rights are!)
I get "stepped on" often.
I'm meek, mile-mannered and very accommodating.

WELCOME

I would describe my communication style as

_____

_____

_____

As a result of my passivity/aggressiveness, I have/am still experiencing the following negative results:

_____

_____

_____

Passive/Aggressive Behavior	Negative Results

One change I need to make in the way I communicate is

_____

_____

_____

One person in my life I will try this week to be more assertive with is

_____

_____

_____

An I-statement can be defined as communication of thoughts or feelings beginning with the word *I*. Even if in the course of an argument you are 100% right and the other person is 100% wrong (which is rarely the case), using the word *you* can put people on the defensive. Arguments often escalate not because we were "wrong" or had an invalid or inferior point of view, but because of how we communicated our point of view. Although it is easy to disagree about interpretation of the facts, it is hard to argue (although some will try) with how someone feels. The following formula can be used to reframe your thoughts into I-statements:

1. What is the problem behavior?

2. Why didn't I like it? How did I feel when it happened?

3. What would I like the person to do instead next time?

Although people are certainly *responsible* for various behaviors, *blaming* them is rarely helpful. Nobody thrives in an atmosphere of blame. The most helpful approach, then, is to assertively communicate what you see the problem to be (without labeling or name calling) and shift quickly to an action request; that is, what you would like the person to do next? Depending on the communication style you identified for yourself in the previous tool, this may present different challenges for you. For instance, many who have a passive style (and an undeserving belief) may think, "I don't have a right to request something of someone else." Conversely, people who have a more aggressive style (and perhaps entitlement beliefs and probably struggle with anger) may think, "She owes it to me—I'll make her give it to me" or thoughts of that nature. So, while some may have difficulty *mustering up* the nerve to communicate in I-statements, others are presented with the task of *calming down* enough to communicate in I-statements.

The following questions are designed to assist you as you develop this important tool:

Three problems in current relationships are:

1.

2.

3.

Using an I-statement, what would be an assertive way to communicate a problem to the other person?

_____

_____

_____

This week, I will practice assertive communication with _____

Occasionally, writing an assertive letter to someone making use of I-statements is helpful. Some people write letters with no intention of mailing them. Others write a "venting" version and then modify it to send a less-aggressive version, and still others are comfortable sending initial versions to the person. It is important to have a therapist or wise friend read the letter to before sending it to receive feedback regarding its appropriateness for achieving your goals.

Marsha Linehan, a faculty member at the University of Washington who developed a treatment called Dialectical Behavior Therapy, identified three important aspects of effective communication that can serve as a helpful format for improving communication skills (Linehan, 1993). She called these *interpersonal effectiveness* skills and identified three different types of effectiveness: *objective effectiveness*, *relationship effectiveness*, and *self-respect effectiveness*. The information in this tool was adapted from *Cognitive-Behavioral Treatment of Borderline Personality Disorder* by Marsha M. Linehan, 1991.

Objective effectiveness refers to obtaining your objective, or getting what you want or need in a given situation. Many people have legitimate wants or needs; however, they simply go about achieving them in an ineffective way when overcome with intense emotions. That is, their goals are fine, but the way they go about getting what they want doesn't work.

Describe a need or want that you have now and answer these questions:

What do I really want?

_____

_____

In the past, what things have I tried that didn't work to get what I wanted?

_____

_____

_____

What were the results of my attempts? _____

_____

_____

What would be the worst way to go about getting what I really want? What would make it least likely for me to get what I want?

_____

_____

_____

What would be the best way to go about getting what I really want?

_____

_____

_____

Relationship effectiveness is the art of maintaining or improving relationships while you are attempting to get what you want or need.

Think back to the relationship cycles in which you examined how your behavior affected someone else. Maintaining relationships effectively requires that you act in a way that influences others to like you while you are attempting to get what you want or need.

Relationships I have lost or damaged in the past by acting ineffectively while attempting to get what I want or need include

_____

_____

_____

Some of the behaviors that were ineffective that I used to get what I wanted or needed were

_____

_____

_____

Behaviors that may be more effective that I could try next time might be

_____

_____

_____

Self-respect effectiveness involves maintaining good feelings about yourself while going about attempting to get what you want or need.

As previously discussed, all humans act less rationally and demonstrate less self-control when their emotions are running high. People who find themselves in difficult and unhealthy relational situations often struggle with self-esteem issues to begin with. Then, when they get emotional and do or say something they regret later, it reinforces their unhealthy core beliefs about themselves, such as "I am bad," or "I can't do anything right." Self-respect effectiveness allows us to go about trying to get what we want in a way that we will feel good about and respect ourselves when the interaction is over, *regardless of whether we achieved our objective.*

One time I felt guilty or lost respect for myself after an argument with someone I cared about was

_____

_____

_____

Things I did or said in that altercation that contributed to my losing respect for myself were

_____

_____

_____

How do I want to feel about myself after my next confrontation with a loved one?

_____

_____

_____

Things I could do or say differently that might help me feel better about myself might be

_____

_____

_____

Consider the following example, identifying what might be helpful for each type of effectiveness.

Example event: Visitation of children limited after divorce

Objective Effectiveness: Questions to Ask

What do I really want? Increased visitation

What things have I done in the past in situations when I felt I was wronged that got me in trouble that I want to make sure NOT to do again?
Make threats and fire off impulsive texts and emails that were used against me

What can I do this time that may be more effective?
Breathe, set limit with myself not to send anything that could incriminate me, call someone to vent, begin to document my case as to why I deserve equal visitation, retain an attorney who can "fight" for me and is trained to do so in a professional way

Relationship Effectiveness: Questions to Ask

How do I want him to feel about me after this is over?
Part of me doesn't care, but I know for the sake of our children, it needs to be civil. I also don't want to let him get the best of me and let him see that.

What do I usually do in these instances that I don't want to do this time?
Threaten, try to punish him in some way

What can I do differently this time?
Remain calm, do nothing immediately, try to be cordial

Self Respect Effectiveness: Questions to Ask

How do I want to feel about myself after this is over?
Like a good parent and a good person, not guilty, empowered

What do I usually do in these instances that I don't want to do this time?
Something impulsive

What can I do differently this time?
Identify my values that are important not to violate, recognize that when I behave in ways that violate those values I feel guilty and embarrassed, live in a way that is consistent with my values

Values that I have that are important for me not to compromise include:

On the introductory page of this chapter, you might note that one of the common beliefs involved in communication difficulties is that *undeserving* belief. People with this belief often believe they don't have a right to communicate assertively in relationships. Tool 18 is less of a behavioral tool and more of a cognitive tool. To the extent that you have that undeserving belief, these statements may be difficult for you to hear. However to improve your assertiveness and general communication skills, gradually allowing yourself to believe these statements can be a most powerful tool. If these ideas don't seem natural to you, try to recite them on a daily basis. If you continue to struggle, utilize your "add a but" tool from Chapter 1. Pick five of the following statements that resonate with you (the ones that are the hardest to "hear" are the ones that likely will benefit you the most) and work on making them your personal bill of rights.

Personal Bill of Rights

1. I have the right to make my own choices.

2. I have the right to follow my own values or standards.

3. I have the right to grieve over my losses.

4. I have the right to say no to anything I don't want to do.

5. I have the right to determine my priorities.

6. I have the right to end conversations I believe are not good for me.

7. I have the right to make mistakes.

8. I have the right to all my feelings.

9. I have the right to be angry with someone I love.

10. I have the right to feel scared.

11. I have the right to be loved.

12. I have the right to change my mind.

13. I have the right to be responsible for my own actions.

14. I have the right not to be responsible for the actions of others.

15. I have the right to stability.

16. I have the right to be relaxed and playful and to have fun.

17. I have the right to be flexible.

18. I have the right to experience fear.

19. I have the right to let go of fear.

20. I have the right to trust.

21. I have the right to change and grow.

22. I have the right to take care of myself.

23. I have the right to forgive.

24. I have the right to be happy.

25. I have the right to be healthy.

My Personal Bill of Rights

1.

2.

3.

4.

5.

The reality is that most people have more control over their "circles" of friends and acquaintances than they believe they have. Actually, for people with "control issues," their problem is often exactly the opposite of not having any control: They don't have as much control as they think they "should."

We do have a significant ability to influence our circles, but we cannot control other people. Depending on your personality, you may be the type of person who could benefit from taking the initiative to improve your circles. Or, you may be a person who would be better served by stopping trying to control others. The following tool will help you examine how to take control of your circles in a way that will be more beneficial for you.

What general observations do you have when looking at your circles? _____

_____

_____

What changes would you like to make to your circles? _____

_____

_____

Who are the people you would like to have closer in? Further out? _____

_____

_____

One person in my circles I could be more compassionate with is _____

One person in my circle I need to be more assertive with is _____

One person in my circle I need to get better at saying *no* to is _____

One person in my circle I can have fun with is _____

One person in my circle I can't talk about serious things with is _____

One person in my life I need to stop trying to control is _____

One thing I need to accept about someone in my circle if I don't want to stay bitter is

_____

_____

One person in my circles I need to say thank you to is _____

One person in my circles I need to apologize to is _____

One person in my circle I'd like to try to spend more time with is _____

Some hurtful things I have done in the past that have damaged one or more
relationships are _____

_____

_____

Some things I have done in the past that have been helped me in maintaining
relationships are

_____

_____

Changes I could make in the way I relate to people may include _____

_____

_____

One small step I am willing to take today to start this process is

_____

_____

The next time I need to communicate an important message to someone, instead of _bullying him/her_____ (go to coping skill, Tool 4),

I can:

1. _ask nicely_____

2. _wait for a better time_____

3. _put it in writing and allow them time to think about it_
   a while

The next time I need to communicate an important message to someone, instead of _____ (go to coping skill, Tool 4),

I can:

1. _____

2. _____

3. _____

Cognitive Cue Card

Just because _I don't always get my way_ **doesn't mean** _I have no say in the_

relationship. My needing to alway be in control has hurt the relationship and I want

to help it.

Cognitive Cue Card

Just because_____(unhelathy coping skill from tool 4),

doesn't mean _____(unhealthy belief),

I know_____(healthy belief), **because**_____

_____

Chapter 6 **Codependency**

COMMON BELIEFS

- Dependence
- Self-Sacrifice
- Emotional deprivation
- Burden

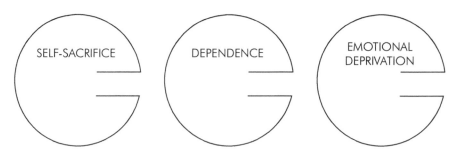

COMMON DISTORTIONS

- "Shoulding" self
- Personalization
- Fortune telling, mind-reading, magnification
- Rationalization

COMMON AUTOMATIC THOUGHTS

- "It is my job to rescue her."
- "If I don't help her, who will?"
- "It's OK to help him because he needs it."
- "If I don't help, it means I'm a bad person."
- "Giving means always helping."
- "It is none of my business what he/she does with what I give."
- "I don't have to be responsible because someone will always have my back."
- "Because I'm her son, she has to help me."

COMMON FEELINGS

- Guilt
- Anxiety
- Helplessness

COMMON BEHAVIORS

- Asking for help
- "Rescuing"
- Dating "bad boys" or others who need "fixing"

Triggers for codependency are more specific than previous relational triggers that we have addressed. It is important to note that many people misuse the term *codependent*. In treatment programs, for example, people commonly say, "I'm so codependent," or "she's so codependent." Codependency inherently involves at least two people, so no one person can be codependent. Codependency describes a type of relationship cycle related to individual needs.

The *dependent* in the relationship is the "taker." The *enabler* in the relationship is the "giver." Enablers typically view themselves as the more healthy of the two, but the reality is that they are just as dysfunctional as the people they are trying to "fix." Enablers often rationalize their caretaking by saying things like, "It's OK to help because they'd be dead without me," or "It's OK to help because that's the nice/admirable/Christian" thing to do." Helping in and of itself can be noble; however, there is a difference between "healthy helping" and "unhealthy helping" that this chapter will help you explore. Because this dynamic involves two people, your triggers will vary depending on whether you are the enabler or the dependent.

If you are the dependent, your triggers may involve things such as neediness, asking for help, asking for substances, asking for money, letting your mom do you your laundry even though you are 40 years old and still living at home. If you are the enabler, your triggers may include "helping" others. You may view them as sick, incapable, or irresponsible. They may be involved with alcohol, drugs, or making poor decisions, or you may be the parent who has made it easy for your adult child to not become responsible. Spend a few minutes and try to identify your triggers for codependency.

I view myself as the _____ **in the codependent cycle.**

I know I am the enabler/dependent [circle one] because _____

_____.

Areas I ask for help/am irresponsible in are _____

_____.

The person in my life I am most likely to rescue is _____.

My triggers for codependency are:

1.

2.

3.

4.

5.

Emotions in the "anxiety family" and guilt are the feelings most frequently experienced by enablers. Dependents often feel helplessness, hopelessness, or even anger in response to denial of caretaking. *Refer to your face sheet* (Tool 2 in Chapter 2) to identify what feelings related to codependence you frequently experience.

My codependency-related feelings are:

1.

2.

3.

4.

5.

The following questions are designed to help you identify your distorted thoughts specifically related to codependency.

When _____ (trigger; see **Tool 1 in this chapter**) **happens,**

and I feel _____ (feelings; see **Tool 2 in this chapter**),

what am I usually telling myself?

If I were in a cartoon, what would the bubble above my head be saying?

If there were a tape recorder in my head recording my every thought, what would it be saying when someone pushed "play?"

Example

I felt ...	...because I thought...
Anxious	If I don't help him, he'll never make it — I can't stand the thought of him suffering.
Guilty	If I don't help him, I'm a bad mom/grandparent/Christian.
Convinced/Compelled (to give $)	It's OK to help him because it's my fault for choosing such a lousy husband who never taught our son how to be responsible.

Thoughts/Feelings Awareness Log

I felt ...	...because I thought...

"Autopilot" unhealthy coping skills in the realm of codependency typically fit into one of two categories, depending on which role you take on. Dependents' go-to skills involve instinctively asking for someone else to support their bad habit (although they don't usually view it as bad). Enablers' coping skills involve some form of helping. Common examples include giving money, giving rides, and parents arguing with teachers to prevent their child from experiencing consequences. Spend a few minutes trying to identify unhealthy behavior habits you may have developed in response to these feelings.

When I feel an impulse to help/ask for help, in the past I have _____

_____

Other things I have done in the past in an attempt to cope that have in some way hurt me are _____

_____

_____

_____

_____

Some of my "go-to"/"autopilot" codependency coping skills are (helping behaviors if you are the enabler; help-seeking behaviors if you are the dependent):

1.

2.

3.

4.

5.

As Tool 4 touched on, things that worked in the past don't always work in the present, and things that work in the present in the short term don't always work in the long term. To increase your awareness, try to identify some of the consequences of your unsuccessful attempted solutions to codependent relationships in the past.

Example

Autopilot Coping Skill (from Tool 4)	Current or Past Negative Consequences
Never imposed consequences on son when he was a child	In jail at age 16 because he grew up to believe rules didn't apply to him
Continued to give daughter money when she couldn't pay her rent without accountability	Daughter died of drug overdose.

Awareness of Consequences Log

Autopilot Coping Skill (from Tool 4)	Current or Past Negative Consequences

Some things I will try to break my codependent cycle are:

1.

2.

3.

4.

5.

Challenging distorted thoughts doesn't always make them go away, but it can put up enough of a "fight" that feelings aren't quite so intense making it at least slightly easier to use some of the skills you identified in Tool 6. Utilize the following *thought log* to attempt to *challenge* or generate some more *rational responses* to the distorted thoughts you identified in Tool 3.

Example

Distorted Thought	Rational Response
If I don't help him, he'll never make it—I can't stand the thought of him suffering.	I've been helping him for 10 years and he isn't any closer to making it now than he was when I started. I have to start viewing pain as a gift—some people have to hit bottom before they learn their lesson. If I have to worry myself sick for him to learn, I'm willing to do it.
If I don't help him, I'm a bad mom/grandparent/Christian.	There is much evidence I am a good mother/grandparent/Christian. Setting boundaries is really a way of helping him whether he sees it now or not.
It's OK to help him because it's my fault for choosing such a lousy husband who never taught our son how to be responsible.	Helping him in this way this long teaches him that he doesn't have to be responsible. I want him to be successful in life, so I don't want to raise him to be like his dad.

Thought Log

Distorted Thought	Rational Response

As a refresher, *core beliefs* are deeply engrained beliefs that serve as filters through which we process information. All of our distorted thinking is the product of one or more harmful beliefs. This technique asks us to take a thought and continue to ask, "What would that mean about us if it were true?" until we get at the core belief is at the bottom of the distorted thought. If necessary, refer back to earlier in the chapter to note beliefs that often contribute to codependent behaviors. Also, remember that many people need a therapist's help to assist with this for a period of time.

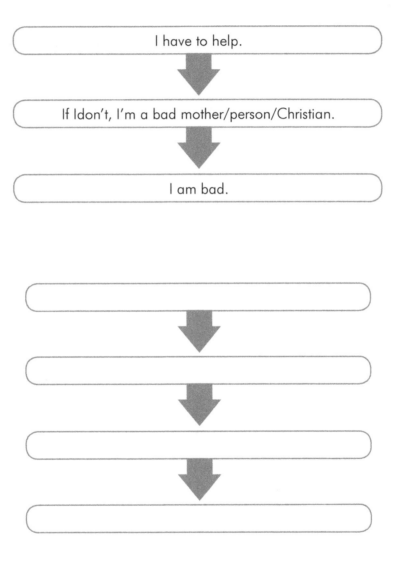

Remember, beliefs come in pairs. For each unhealthy belief you identified, formulate in your words what the exact opposite of that would mean to you. Flexible language remains important.

Example

My Beliefs

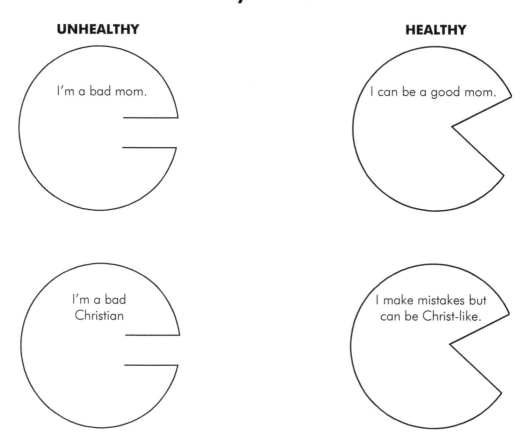

UNHEALTHY

I'm a bad mom.

I'm a bad Christian

HEALTHY

I can be a good mom.

I make mistakes but can be Christ-like.

My Beliefs

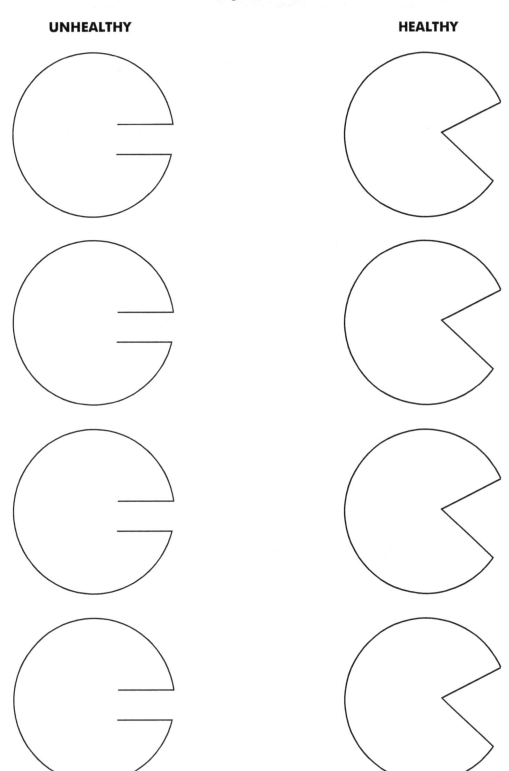

UNHEALTHY

HEALTHY

The strength of our beliefs significantly influences how often we feel stressful emotions and how strongly we experience them. Take a few minutes and try to assign a strength to each healthy and unhealthy belief. Usually, the easiest way is to use percentages so the total for unhealthy and healthy beliefs equals 100 percent.

Example

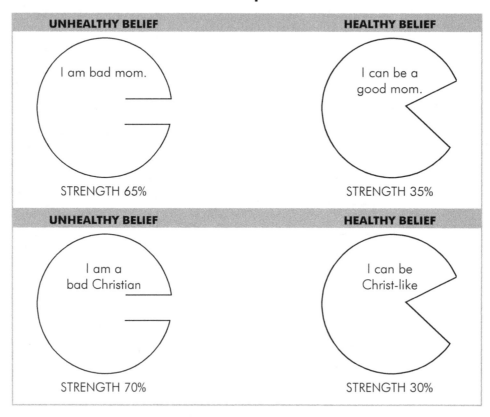

Rating the Strength of My Beliefs

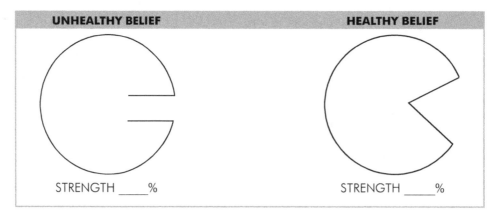

The following questions may be helpful in reflecting back on different periods of life to uncover some of the experiences you counted as evidence to support your belief (legs to hold up your table). You may need assistance from your therapist to get the most out of this tool.

The first time I ever remember feeling _____[belief]

was _____

The people in my life who influenced me to feel that way were:

Family members _____

_____

Friends/Peers _____

_____

Other significant people _____

_____

Experiences during my elementary school years _____

_____

_____

Experiences during my junior high years _____

_____

_____

Experiences during my high school years _____

_____

_____

Experiences during my college/young adult years _____

_____

_____

Significant experiences since then _____

_____

_____

Use the exercise on the previous page to try to insert some of the "evidence" from your past that you have "counted" to support each belief:

Example

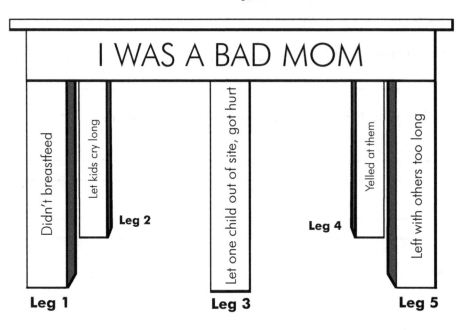

Evidence that I was a bad mom:

Leg 1: I didn't breastfeed.

Leg 2: I let them cry longer than I should have.

Leg 3: I let one child out of my sight and she swallowed something dangerous.

Leg 4: I yelled at them.

Leg 5: I left them to be cared for by others too often.

Unhealthy Evidence Log

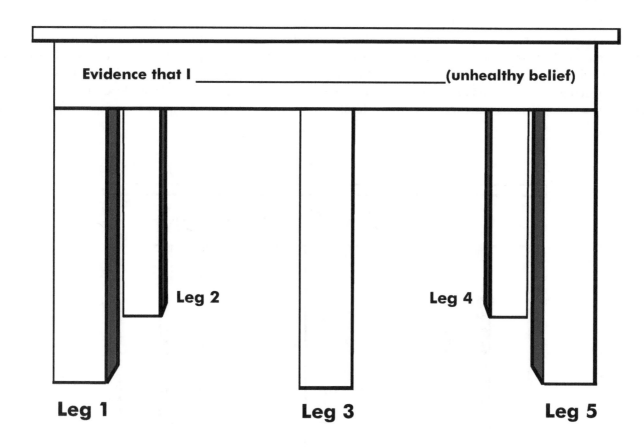

Evidence that I _____(unhealthy belief)

Leg 1

Leg 2

Leg 3

Leg 4

Leg 5

Leg 1:

Leg 2:

Leg 3:

Leg 4:

Leg 5:

Because of how our filters are set up, we often notice instances that support the unhealthy beliefs more than we notice experiences that may support our opposite, healthy beliefs, but almost always, that "evidence" exists as well. One valuable tool involves forcing ourselves to look back over those very same periods of life purposefully looking to see the evidence that supports our healthy beliefs. Many people rely on family members or friends who were around them during each period of life to help them remember and "notice" such evidence. Even if they share things they see as "counting" that you don't think should "count," write them down anyway—- a tool to help with that is provided later!

Example

CAN BE A GOOD MOM

They always have food

Always have clothes

Leg 2

Told them they are loved

Got them involved

Leg 4

Left them in good hands

Leg 1

Leg 3

Leg 5

Evidence that I can be a good mom:

Leg 1: They always had food.

Leg 2: They always had clothes.

Leg 3: I told them I loved them often.

Leg 4: I got them involved in activities early.

Leg 5: I made sure they were in good hands when I was unavailable.

Healthy Evidence Log

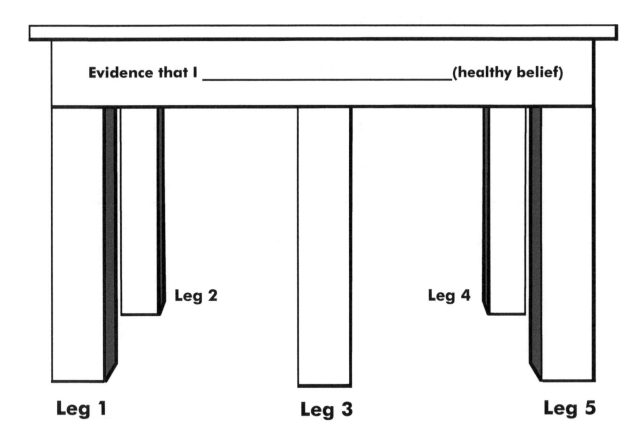

Evidence that I _____ (healthy belief)

Leg 1

Leg 2

Leg 3

Leg 4

Leg 5

Leg 1:

Leg 2:

Leg 3:

Leg 4:

Leg 5:

Beliefs *mean* different things to different people. Refer to Tool 13 in Chapter 2 for examples of what it might mean to *have value*. Using that as a guide, compile a list of a few things that support your healthy beliefs about yourself.

Example

Belief	**Components**
1. Can be good mom	**1.** Physical needs of kids met
	2. Emotional needs of kids met
	3. Social needs of kids met

Belief	**Components**
1.	**1.**
	2.
	3.
2.	**1.**
	2.
	3.
3.	**1.**
	2.
	3.

Purposefully pay attention to things in life that might count as evidence that your healthy belief could be true.

Example

Evidence that I can be a good mom

Date	Evidence
3/6	Went to parent-teacher conference
3/13	Helped with homework
3/17	Prepared a healthy meal
3/18	Went for a family walk
3/22	Talked about "boy problems"

I CAN BE A
GOOD MOM

Evidence that I can be _____ (healthy belief) log

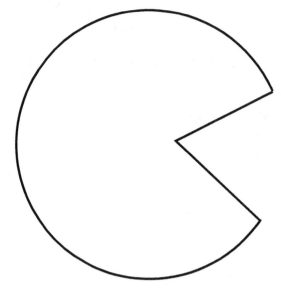

Date	Evidence

Codependency, as previously stated, describes a type of relationship, not a single person. Thus, assessing whether you have an issue with codependency requires considering your potential "dependent" qualities as well as your potential "enabler" traits. The following tests in Tool 15 will help you assess your qualities in each of these areas. Rate each of these on a scale of 0 to 5 using the following key, then total your scores. Scores of 30 or higher may signify issues in these areas.

1 = This seems never to be true of me.

2 = This seems rarely to be true of me.

3 = This sometimes is true of me.

4 = This seems often to be true of me.

5 = This seems always to be true of me.

Assessing My Dependent Traits

I tend to rely on others to meet my needs.	1 2 3 4 5
I have difficulty initiating tasks on my own.	1 2 3 4 5
I seem to require a lot of reassurance when making decisions.	1 2 3 4 5
I have difficulty disagreeing with friends or dating partners.	1 2 3 4 5
I say yes a lot when I'd like to say no.	1 2 3 4 5
Others have described me as "needy" or "clingy."	1 2 3 4 5
I fear others may leave me and I'll be left to fend for myself.	1 2 3 4 5
I have to be in a romantic relationship to feel complete.	1 2 3 4 5

Total: _____

Assessing My Enabler Traits

1 = This seems never to be true of me.

2 = This seems rarely to be true of me.

3 = This sometimes is true of me.

4 = This seems often to be true of me.

5 = This seems always to be true of me.

I feel responsible for other people.   1 2 3 4 5

I feel anxiety or guilt when others have a problem.   1 2 3 4 5

I feel compelled to help people solve their problems.   1 2 3 4 5

I often over-commit myself.   1 2 3 4 5

It is much easier for me to give than receive.   1 2 3 4 5

I find myself attracted to needy people.   1 2 3 4 5

Needy people find themselves attracted to me.   1 2 3 4 5

I feel like the choices of others drive me crazy.   1 2 3 4 5

Total: _____

As previously mentioned, undeserving, emotional deprivation, and burden beliefs keep people from experiencing intimacy with others and getting needs met. Intimacy involves both giving and receiving. Receiving requires being able to ask for and accept help. Before you can ask, however, you must know what your needs are. People who grew up in families where it was "weak" to have needs or unacceptable to acknowledge needs may not even know what their needs are. Tool 16 can help you identify some of your needs so when you get to the next tools you'll know what to ask for! This is by no means an exhaustive list, but hopefully it will get you going in the right direction.

Physical Needs	Emotional Needs	Relationship Needs
Food	Feeling safe/secure	Being affirmed/validated
Water	Feeling loved	Being served in some way
Shelter	Feeling cared for	Quality time with others
Clothing	Feeling respected	Being included/feeling heard
Physical touch	Finding meaning/purpose	Willingness to compromise

Other needs:

Some of my needs are:

1.

2.

3.

4.

5.

Asking for and accepting help are two different things. If it is difficult for you to ask for help, probably once you ask it, will feel uncomfortable when others offer. Here is why many people don't ask for the help they need—they don't want to have to deal with the uncomfortable feelings that could come from having to receive it. As you look at your list of needs, you might note that some needs are more appropriately met by certain people than others. If you identified sexual needs, it is obviously most appropriate and healthy for those to be met by a spouse or partner. Other needs, such as to share events of a very personal nature, may be met by a therapist or close friend. Some people identify needs along the lines of "intellectual stimulation," or "camaraderie/fun." These needs can be met by people in your outer circles. You can enjoy a movie, lecture, or nightclub with people you don't necessarily trust with your deepest secrets. Thus, identifying what needs could potentially be met by whom can be an important step. Tool 17 will help you identify whom you could potentially ask for what and will help you work on accepting that help when you ask.

Example

My Need	Person Who Could Potentially Meet Need
Discuss spiritual concerns	Campus chaplain
Discuss past abuse	Therapist
Get dating advice	Therapist, two close friends
Have intellectual stimulation	Debate team
Have fun	Sorority sisters

My Need	Person Who Could Potentially Meet Need

Finally, part of being human means sometimes having unmet needs. Some people struggle with the distorted thought, "I must get all my needs met—It is unacceptable if I don't." If this is you, one of your tough tasks will be learning to accept that we all have unmet needs at various points in life.

Unmet needs I have at this point in my life are _____

_____

_____

_____

If you struggle with accepting help, it can be useful to notice and track your reactions and responses to help as people begin to offer it. Continue to work to improve your comfort level with accepting help. When you are able to accept help, give yourself credit. When your reaction is to turn down an offer of help in some way, ask yourself, "Could I have responded differently in a way that would have helped me receive help/get a need met more effectively?"

Date	Help Offered	My Response	What I Could Do Differently to Receive Help Better Next Time

Regardless of whether you saw yourself as the "enabler" or the "dependent," if you notice yourself getting stuck in this cycle, you have issues related to dependence. Often, enablers view themselves as the more independent partner in the relationship. But the reality is, enablers are just as dependent as "dependents." Independent people don't thrive on this dynamic. They don't get caught up in these "messes." They would rather have nothing to do with "relational drama." Thus, anyone that has dependent traits and finds himself or herself in either of these roles could benefit from becoming a little more independent. Developing independence is not an easy process, but the results are often experienced as highly rewarding for those who are willing to pursue growth in this area. Tool 18 will assist you in getting started with this process.

Tips for Developing Independence

1. Stop relying on others to be happy.

2. Develop an identity that is independent of others.

3. Identify and develop relationships so that others can meet some of your needs.

4. Identify and develop strategies for meeting some of your own needs.

5. Learn to rely on God to meet some needs.

Stop Relying on Others For Your Happiness

People in my life I have been relying on for my happiness are _____

_____

_____

_____

Steps I am willing to take to detach from those people are _____

_____

_____

_____

Develop an Identity Independent of Others

Some of the things in my life I enjoy that are in no way tied to my relationships to others are

_____

_____

_____

Hobbies or interests I have enjoyed in the past or think I might enjoy getting involved with include _____

_____

_____

Causes or values I believe to be important include

_____

_____

_____

Specific steps I am willing to take to pursue involvement with these include:

1.

2.

3.

Identify and Develop Relationships so that Others Can
Meet Some of Your Needs

Needs I have that others can meet are (draw from Tool 17): _____

_____

_____

_____

Identify and Develop Strategies for Meeting Some of Your Own Needs

Evidence that I can be OK on my own includes (review evidence logs from earlier tool for expanded version of this):

Date	Evidence That I Can Be OK or Meet My Needs on My Own

Learn to Rely on God to Meet Some Needs

My spiritual beliefs can help provide a sense of emotional security for me in the following ways_____

_____

_____

God can help meet the following needs in my life:

_____

_____

_____

God can help me deal with and learn to accept unmet needs in my life in the following ways:

_____

_____

Previous tools have discussed the need to set boundaries or limits with others. Some people actually benefit more from being able to set limits with themselves! Depending on whether you saw yourself as the "dependent" or the "enabler," the types of limits you may benefit from setting with yourself may vary. The following tool will help you identify some of these limits and get a good start in that direction.

Dependent

- Resist the urge to ask for help.
- Notice that "autopilot/default" voice in your head that says, *"I can't."* Remind yourself that you have in the past and you *can.*
- Pay attention to that voice that tells you not to try. Take initiative/start something anyway even though it doesn't feel natural.
- Resist the temptation to call a toxic relationship partner. Notice the voice that says you need him or her. Reach out to healthy people, God, or find ways to meet the need yourself! Create evidence that you don't need the toxic partner, even though you may feel in that moment that you do.

Enabler

- Increase your awareness of your feelings of anxiety when you see others with a problem.
- Allow yourself to feel empathy, or even sympathy, but not guilt. Remind yourself that you are not responsible for others.
- Resist the urge to help.
- Realize that although you intend it to be "help," it may not be helping the other person. It may be meeting a need in you but keeping him or her sick or stuck.
- Allow others to suffer the consequences of their actions. Realize that pain can be a gift and you may be robbing them of a learning experience if you can't resist your need to rescue.
- Practice saying no.

Limits I Will Set with Myself Include:

1.

2.

3.

4.

5.

Coping Cards

The next time I catch myself wanting to enable_____(name),

instead of _____ (enabling behavior, Tool 4),

I will:

1. _____

2. _____

3. _____

The next time I catch myself wanting to ask somebody for help, instead first I will try:

1. _____

2. _____

3. _____

Cognitive Cue Cards

Just because _I say no_

doesn't _make me a bad person ....my saying yes actually robs them_

them of an opportunity to grow.

Just because I say now doesn't mean_____

I know I am a caring person because_____

_____

Chapter 7 **Problem Solving**

COMMON BELIEFS

- Helpless
- Dependent
- Failure

COMMON DISTORTIONS

- Fortune Telling
- Emotional Reasoning
- Rationalization

COMMON AUTOMATIC THOUGHTS

- "I can't do this."
- "I have to ask for help."
- "This feels overwhelming so Why even try"?
- "I've tried everything, nothing works."

COMMON FEELINGS

- Helplessness
- Anxiety
- Inadequacy
- Hopelessness

COMMON BEHAVIORS

- Give up
- Try, but give 1/2 effort so fail
- Ask for help without trying
- Try "extreme" option rather than more effective one

Problem solving triggers are unique from the other areas we've covered in the sense that they only arise when one has a problem to deal with. Some think of a problem as a major life obstacle, but it can be helpful to think of a "problem" as any situation in which one has a decision to make. Consider areas for problem solving triggers in your life:

I typically have problems to deal with in the following areas:

- Problems with friends
- Problems in my marriage
- Problems in my dating relationships
- Problems with parents
- Problems with children
- Problems with siblings
- Problems with extended family
- Problems related to money/financial decisions
- Problems related to church
- Problems related to volunteer work
- Problems dealing with a supervisor
- Problems dealing with peers at work
- Problems with my sex life
- Problems related to parenting style disagreements
- Problems during vacation or travel
- Problems related to use of alcohol or drugs
- Problems related to work related stress
- Problems related to physical health/medical decisions

The last time I had a problem to solve was _____.

The area I had a problem in most recently was _____.

The areas I usually have problems in most are _____.

Themes in problems I have seem to be _____.

My problem-solving triggers are:

1.

2.

3.

4.

5.

Some people are very good at expressing their feelings. Others have difficulty recognizing, giving names to, or even recognizing that they have feelings at all. The "Feelings Face Sheet" included in Tool 2 in Chapter 2 is often helpful for aiding people in identifying what feelings they are actually having. Using the face sheet as your guide, pick out several feelings that seem to describe best what you experience when you are facing a problem in life.

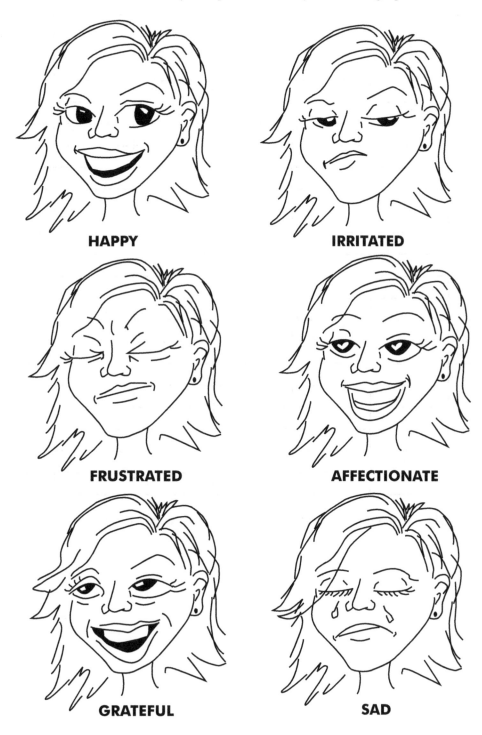

HAPPY　　　　　　　**IRRITATED**

FRUSTRATED　　　　　**AFFECTIONATE**

GRATEFUL　　　　　　**SAD**

Feelings Log

Type of Feeling	Mon	Tues	Wed	Thurs	Fri	Sat	Sun
Happy							
Sad							
Excited							
Angry							
Irritated							
Frustrated							
Proud							
Regretful							
Disgusted							
Excited							
Guilty							
Ashamed							
Anxious							
Confident							
Resentful							
Gloomy							
Fearful							
Scared							
Panicked							
Grateful							
Loved							
Envious							
Jealous							
Compassionate							
Affectionate							

Feelings I typically experience when confronted with a problem are:

1.

2.

3.

4.

5.

Some therapists may use the term *irrational thoughts*. Others prefer the term *dysfunctional thoughts* or *maladaptive thoughts*. The advantage of thinking of thoughts as dysfunctional is recognizing that thoughts that were functional or helpful in one setting may become dysfunctional or hurtful in other settings. For instance, someone who grew up in an abusive family might have learned through experience that, "If I speak up, somebody gets hit or yelled at, or someone leaves, so it's best that I just never speak up." Now, if someone really did get hurt every time he opened his mouth, it would be adaptive to keep his mouth shut. But, if that person adopts that way of thinking ("It's best that I just keep my mouth shut") even after he has grown up and left that home, it is not functional or adaptive and will not lead to effective outcomes. Thus, what is functional in one setting is not necessarily helpful in other contexts. Other professionals may use the term *distorted thinking*. This is the term this workbook uses. Distorted thoughts might be defined as any thoughts that in get in the way of our feeling and behaving in healthy manners.

The following questions are designed to help you identify your distorted thoughts specifically related to low self-esteem:

When _____(trigger; see **Tool 1 in this chapter**) **happens,**

and I feel _____(feelings; see **Tool 2 in this chapter**),

what am I usually telling myself?

If I were in a cartoon, what would the bubble above my head be saying?

If there were a tape recorder in my head recording my every thought, what would it be saying when someone pushed "play?"

Example

I felt ...	...because I thought...
Intimidated	This seems impossible.
Helpless	I can't do this.
Anxious	What if I can't solve this? Something terrible may happen.

Thoughts/Feelings Awareness Log

I felt ...	...because I thought...

Most people develop a set of standard "go-to" coping skills when they are confronted with a problem in their lives. Perhaps you have heard the term *autopilot*, referring to just falling back on the same old skills that in some way feel comfortable but usually don't help. Usually, these behaviors "worked" in the past, but no longer work in the present. Also, some may continue to "work" in the short term but may be making problems worse in the long term. A few such examples include alcohol, drugs, promiscuous sex, spending, or workaholism as methods of not having to face problems. Before figuring out healthy skills to use when these issues come up, it is often useful to generate a list of what we have been trying that has *NOT* been working.

The last time I had a problem communicating, I _____

Other things I have done in the past in an attempt to get through to other people include _____

_____

_____

_____

_____

Example

Some of my "go-to"/"autopilot" problem-solving coping skills are:

1. Shut down
2. Attack/blame someone else
3. Try the first thing that comes to mind

Some of my "go-to"/"autopilot" communication coping skills are:

1.

2.

3.

4.

5.

As Tool 4 touched on, things that worked in the past don't always work in the present, and things that work in the present in the short term don't always work in the long term. Some people have little to no awareness as to how their past coping choices have impacted their present life circumstances. Others fully recognize that their present choices may cause future consequences but continue to choose that "quick feel-good" behavior regardless. One tool that often helps motivate people to change is taking a close look at how their past behaviors have contributed to present undesirable situations. When considering consequences for autopilot behaviors, keep in mind that consequences can take many forms. Areas to consider in your life may include relationships, mood, physical health, financial circumstances, spiritual life, and occupational satisfaction, to name just a few. Spend a few minutes seeing if you can make some of these connections.

Example

Autopilot Coping Skill (from Tool 4)	Current or Past Negative Consequences
Shut down	Bills piled up, got electricity shut off
Tried first thing thought of	Blew up in my face

Awareness of Consequences Log

Autopilot Coping Skill (from Tool 4)	Current or Past Negative Consequences

Maybe you've heard it said that "Change = Insight + Action." While it is true that many people never develop insight into their unhealthy behaviors, it's also true that many people do develop insight into unhealthy behaviors but never take action to change them! Perhaps you have also heard Albert Einstein's definition of insanity: *doing the same thing over and over again expecting a different result!* For instance, some people recognize that their relationship partner "picker" is broken but continue to select unhealthy men or women to be with. Millions of Americans now recognize that smoking has many health hazards but refuse to quit. The reality is, if we want things to get better in our lives, we have to be willing to try something different! We may try a new skill and find that it doesn't work either, but at least we tried. We can now add it to the list of skills we already know don't work and move on to try something else. It is kind of like trying on new shoes—if one pair doesn't fit, no harm done. We just put them in the pile that won't work for us and keep trying. These coping skills are often more specific to the particular problem you are faced with. Refer to your list of coping skills and pick some things you are willing to try next time you are faced with a problem of some kind.

Some things I will try the next time I am confronted with a problem are:

1.

2.

3.

4.

5.

In the same way that recognizing but continuing unhealthy behaviors rarely gets us far along in recovery, recognizing distorted thoughts but not changing them also keeps us stuck. Recognizing and identifying these thoughts is an important first step, but if we don't rigorously challenge them, we will continue to suffer those same horrible feelings we have about ourselves, which in turn make it more difficult to not revert to those autopilot behaviors. Challenging distorted thoughts doesn't always make them go away, but it can put up enough of a "fight" that feelings aren't quite so intense and it may be at least slightly easier to use some of the skills you identified in Tool 6. Utilize the following thought log to attempt to *challenge* or generate some more *rational responses* to your distorted thoughts you identified in Tool 3.

Example

Distorted Thought	Rational Response
This is impossible.	Just because something seems impossible doesn't mean it is.
I can't do this.	I have believed before that I was able to accomplish things that seemed impossible. Maybe I can. If I try, I at least have a chance — if I don't try, I have zero chance. I can ask for help
What if I can't salve this? Something terrible may happen.	Maybe others can help me solve it. Even if I don't solve this, I will be OK.

Thought Log

Distorted Thought	Rational Response

As mentioned in Chapter 1, *Core Beliefs* are deeply ingrained beliefs that we have in different areas of life (self, others, and the world). They serve as "filters" through which we process information. Because we all have had different life experiences, our filters are unique. It is because of these filters that each of us may perceive things differently. Thus two people can go through the same event and come out of it with a different experience. Filters contribute to different thoughts, feelings, and responses. One tool that can help identify core beliefs is called the *downward arrow* technique. This technique asks us to take a thought and continue to ask "what would that mean about us if it were true?" until we get at what the core belief is at the bottom of the distorted thought. Note the following example, and then try one on your own. Many people need a therapist's help to assist with this for a period of time.

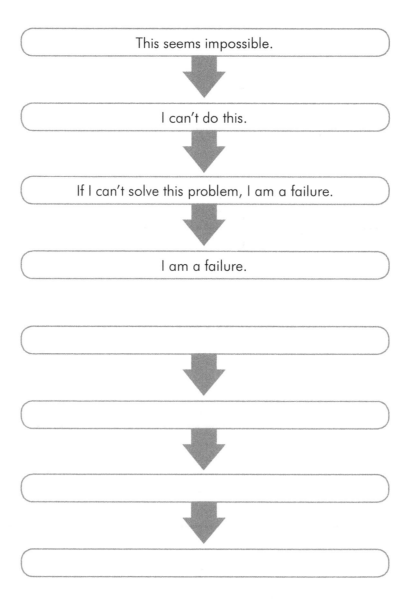

It's similar to when we take our car into the shop: The mechanic never tells us about the 300 and some things that *are working*. He tells us about the one or two that are not, because that is why we had to bring the car in to begin with. Similarly, in therapy, the focus is often on the unhealthy beliefs, but *the reality is that beliefs come in pairs*. For every unhealthy belief, we all have an opposite, healthy belief. For instance, if you identified a self-belief that says, *"I am a failure,"* you may want to identify your opposite healthy belief as something like, *"I can succeed."* Take a few minutes, and for each unhealthy belief you identified using Tool 7, think about how you might want to phrase the opposite of that. Keep in mind that it is helpful to keep beliefs flexible, such as *"can succeed"* rather than *"am always successful."*

Example

My Beliefs

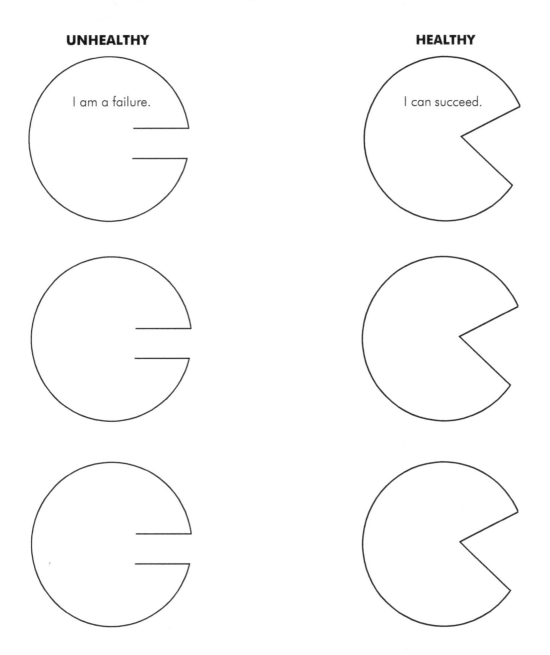

UNHEALTHY — I am a failure.

HEALTHY — I can succeed.

Just because we believe something, doesn't mean we believe it a hundred percent. For instance there are people who are convinced (a 100 percent belief) that there is life on other planets. There are people who are certain there is not (a 0 percent belief). Others may believe it is *possible* but not likely (maybe a 10 percent belief). Similarly, some people believe they are a failure 100 percent of the time and successful 0 percent of the time. Others may see themselves as a failure 70 percent and as successful 30 percent. The strength of our beliefs significantly influences how often we feel certain emotions and how strongly we experience them. Take a few minutes and try to assign a strength to each healthy and unhealthy belief. Usually, the easiest way is to use percentages so the total for unhealthy and healthy beliefs equals 100 percent.

Example

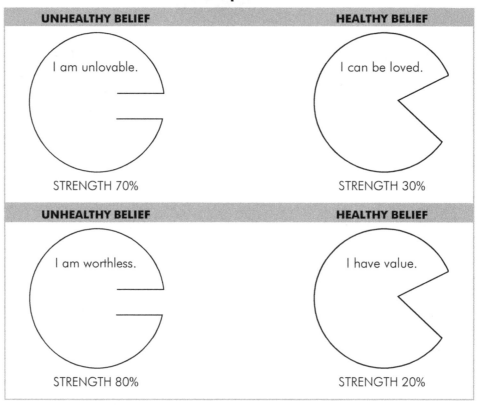

Rating the Strength of My Beliefs

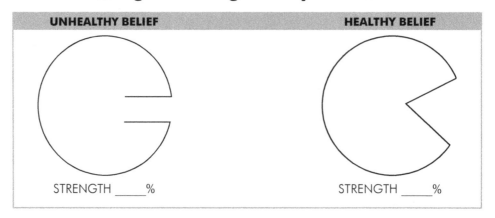

Leslie Sokol, a faculty member at the Beck Institute, compares a belief to a tabletop. In the same way that tabletops need legs to hold them up, beliefs need legs or "evidence" to support them. *"Evidence"* is in quotation marks because different people *count* evidence differently. For instance, some people who believe in aliens may have heard the same stories (information) as people who do not, but for various reasons, one person "counts" it as "evidence" and the other does not. The same holds true for beliefs about ourselves. Anyone who has a failure belief about themselves, whether they realize it or not, has collected "evidence" that they have "counted" over the years to support that belief. This exercise can be a little more time consuming and emotionally draining than some of the previous ones, but it can be a powerful tool for recovery.

The following questions may be helpful in reflecting back on different periods of life to uncover some of the experiences you counted as evidence to support your belief (legs to hold up your table). You may need assistance from your therapist to get the most out of this tool.

The first time I ever remember feeling _____**[belief]**

was _____

The people in my life who influenced me to feel that way were:

Family members _____
_____

Friends/Peers _____
_____

Other significant people _____
_____

Experiences during my elementary school years _____
_____

Experiences during my junior high years _____
_____

Experiences during my high school years _____
_____

Experiences during my college/young adult years _____
_____
_____

Significant experiences since then _____
_____
_____

Use the exercise on the previous page to try to insert some of the "evidence" from your past that you have "counted" to support each belief.

Example

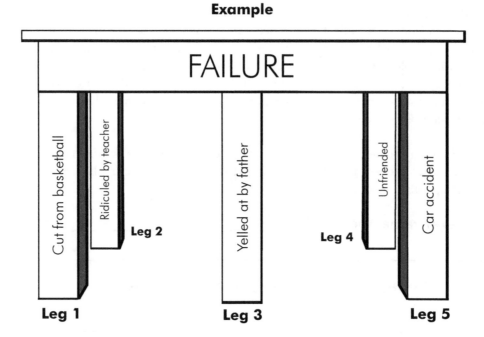

Evidence that I am a failure:

Leg 1: Cut from 8th grade basketball team

Leg 2: Ridiculed for science project by teacher

Leg 3: Father yelled at me in garage for mistake on construction project

Leg 4: Was unfriended by classmate

Leg 5: Got into car accident while texting and driving

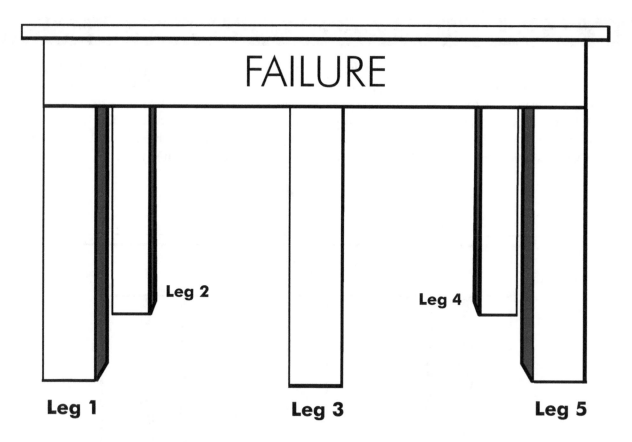

FAILURE

Leg 1   Leg 2   Leg 3   Leg 4   Leg 5

Evidence that I am a failure:

Leg 1:

Leg 2:

Leg 3:

Leg 4:

Leg 5:

Because of how these filters (our beliefs) are set up, we often notice instances that support the unhealthy beliefs more than we notice experiences that may support our opposite, healthy beliefs. But almost always that "evidence" exists as well. One valuable tool involves forcing ourselves to look back over those very same periods of life purposefully looking to see the evidence that supports our healthy beliefs. People often ask family members or friends who were around them during each period of life to help them "notice" such evidence. Even if they share things they see as "counting" that you don't think "should count" write them down anyway.

Example

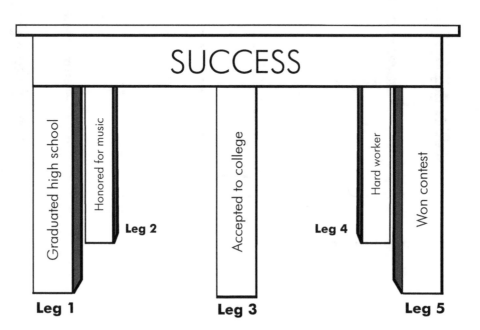

Evidence that I can succeed:

Leg 1: I graduated from high school.

Leg 2: I was honored on numerous occasions for my music.

Leg 3: I was accepted to college.

Leg 4: I am a hard worker and can accomplish much when I put my mind to it.

Leg 5: I won the contest last week.

Healthy Evidence Log

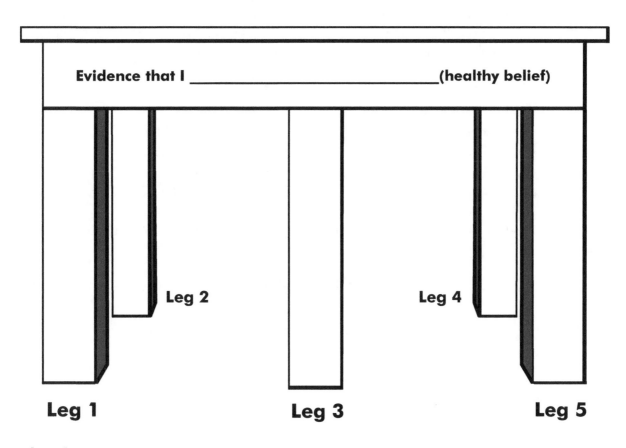

Evidence that I _____(healthy belief)

Leg 1

Leg 2

Leg 3

Leg 4

Leg 5

Leg 1:

Leg 2:

Leg 3:

Leg 4:

Leg 5:

Beliefs mean different things to different people. For instance, people who are working from the unhealthy belief that they are failure have specific ideas as to what that means. Perhaps the opposite healthy belief they are working to build is that they can succeed. People count *accomplishments* differently from *successes* because different things are important to different people. Areas people may perceive as successful include:

- Good grades
- A strong attendance record
- Keeping the house clean
- Work-related projects
- Scientific exploration/advancement
- Promotions

- Salary
- Saving money
- Successful children
- Completing a task
- Finishing a daily "to-do" list
- Cleaning something

Components of the belief of *success* are different to different people. To build healthy beliefs, it is important to identify the *components* of your healthy belief.

Belief

1.

Components

1.

2.

3.

2.

1.

2.

3.

3.

1.

2.

3.

Ongoing evidence logs are another important tool for developing more healthy beliefs and thus becoming less reactive. While previous tools have asked you to review your life and look for "evidence" from the past, ongoing evidence logs ask you to be mindful of evidence in your everyday life. Since your unhealthy filters will naturally be pointing you toward negative evidence, it is often necessary to purposefully seek out positive evidence. *Purposefully seek out* doesn't mean "make it up" if it legitimately isn't there but rather means to try to pay attention to any evidence that legitimately may be present but missed due to your negative filter. It is helpful to collect evidence for each belief you struggle with, but is recommended to pick only one or two to focus on at a given time.

Example

Evidence that I can succeed

Date	Evidence
3/12	Cleaned house
3/13	Found most items on scavenger hunt
3/16	Finished four loads of laundry
3/20	Completed errands
3/22	Won $50 in trivia contest

I CAN SUCCEED

Evidence that I can be _____ (healthy belief) log

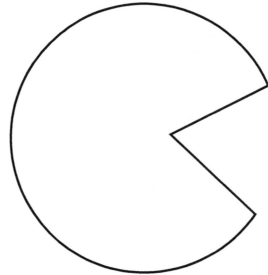

Date	Evidence

To some, this sounds like a "no-brainer," but the first step in addressing problems is creating a problem log. What exactly are the problems you are facing? What is a problem to you often isn't a problem to others. What is a problem to others may not be a problem for you. Some problems are multifaceted, having several dimensions. That is, what may be seen as a single problem may really involve a series of problems: As people like to say, "It's complicated." However, just because a situation is complicated doesn't mean it can't be resolved. Enlist friends, family, or a therapist to help you identify specifically what your problems are and rank them in terms of importance (i.e., 1 = "must solve first," and 3, 4, or 5, depending on how many problems you have, = "can wait").

My Problem Log

1.

2.

3.

4.

5.

Once you have created your problem log and have decided which problem to start with, it is time to start generating options. It is often helpful to generate three to five options, or *things you could do*. This doesn't mean you will do those things; it just gives you a menu of options to choose from. People who struggle with black-and-white thinking often have difficulty even generating options. For instance, one of my patients who was trying to solve the problem of deciding whether to spend Christmas at the home of a family member where she felt uncomfortable was asked in group to generate options. She said, "What do you mean, options? I don't have any!" The group then assured her that she did and challenged her to come up with five. "What do you mean five options?" she said. "I go, or I don't go." Her black-and-white thinking kept her from generating the middle-ground alternatives that the group was then able to help her develop, such as:

1. Not going at all

2. Going for just an hour

3. Going, but telling an aunt who would be there how uncomfortable she was and planning to "hang out mainly with her"

4. Going and staying as long as she could, but leaving as soon as her father was critical

5. Having a friend "on call" to call if things got bad

6. Taking a friend with her

7. Going and staying the whole time no matter what

This list of options the group helped her generate gave her several middle-ground alternatives to just "going or not going." Take a few minutes and consider what your options are. Remember to write them all down even if at first thought you do not think you will choose a particular option.

Five possible things I could do to solve the identified problem are:

1.

2.

3.

4.

5.

This tool asks you to return to your circle of relationships (Tool 15 in Chapter 4) and determine who on your support team may be best suited to assist you with the given problem you are facing. If the problem is related to abuse, a salary issue, or something else more personal, it is probably in your best interest to choose someone in your innermost circle. If it is a problem with your car that you are dealing with, it can be someone in your outer circles who has a mechanical background. If the problem involves a relationship, it may be helpful to call someone who also knows that person. Pick a member of your support team to call and ask them:

- How do you see this problem?
- How might one of my core beliefs be influencing how I see it?
- Here are the options I see. Do you see any others?
- What are the pros and cons of the options I have?

People I could call for advice on this particular problem are:

1.

2.

3.

4.

5.

Tool 18 helps you evaluate the potential pros and cons of each option you generated. We use the term *potential* because we don't know for sure how something will turn out until we try it, but it helps to make educated guesses. Utilize the following table to weigh the potential pros and cons of your options.

	Possible Positive Outcomes (Pros)	**Possible Negative Outcomes (Cons)**
Option 1:		
Option 2:		
Option 3:		
Option 4:		
Option 5:		

Now it is time to choose one option and see what happens! Consider these general tips first:

When presented with a problem, always wait 30 minutes or longer if possible before making a decision. It is almost always acceptable to say, "I need to think about that for a while. When can I get back to you?"

Never make a major life decision while in an episode. Chances are, you won't solve your problem and may make it worse.

After thinking rationally, calming down, and processing with a member of your support team, make the decision you believe to be best for you.

Not all attempts to solve problems work. If a solution doesn't work, don't *"should"* yourself (beat yourself up). Try again. Use the following log to help track your problems and your attempted solutions. Remember to use a different log for different problems, as some attempted solutions that may not work at all for one problem may work splendidly for another.

Take Your Pick!

Problem: _____

Date	Attempted Solution	Ways This Helped	Ways This Didn't Help	Worth Trying Again (Y/N)?

All human beings are able to think more rationally when they are calm. On the flip side, it is more difficult for anyone to think rationally when they are "worked up" or have a "button pushed." So, it makes sense that these are the times our emotions often get the best of us and we make choices that are counterproductive. Wouldn't it be nice if we could think as rationally in the "heat of the moment" as we are able to after we calm down? The reality is that most people have difficulty thinking clearly under pressure. One tool that can assist us in doing better "in the heat of the moment" is flashcards. Coping cards are designed to help us *act* differently in such moments. Cognitive cue cards are designed to help us *think* differently in those situations. So the idea here is, in your calm moments, write down on a 3x5 note card what you believe you need to hear during the less-calm moments.

A coping card always takes the following form:

When I'm tempted to ____*shut down*____ (behavior from Tool 4),

  I can (choices from Tool 6):

   1. Ask my friends to help me gernerate three options for solvng
                                                                    this problem

   2. Weigh the pros and cons of the options _____

   3. Seek advice and try implementing it _____

When I'm tempted to _____ (behavior from Tool 4),

  I can (choices from Tool 6):

   1. _____

   2. _____

   3. _____

A cognitive cue card does not list behaviors but rather takes triggers (Tool 1) and robs them of the negative meaning your critical voice is attempting to give them. Cue cards take the following form:

Just because _____ [trigger] doesn't mean _____ [negative belief].

Challenge negative meaning with neutral or positive meaning:

Example

Cognitive Cue Card

Just because _I shut down and didn't_ **doesn't mean** _I am a failure. I gave in and_
succeed in that moment

avoided this time, but I am making better choices than I was a month ago.

I know _I am successful_ **is true because** _I contrinbute around the_

house, I am pursuing a degree, and I am working toward supporting myself.

Cognitive Cue Card

Just because _____ **doesn't mean** _____

_____

I know _____ **is true because** _____

_____

Chapter 8 **Depression**

COMMON BELIEFS

- Negativity/Pessimism

COMMON DISTORTIONS

- Discounting the Positive/Selective abstraction/Mental filter
- Rationalization

COMMON AUTOMATIC THOUGHTS

- "I always have been depressed, and I always will be depressed."
- "There is no way out."
- "Things will never get better."
- "Its OK to stay in bed because I don't feel like doing anything."

COMMON FEELINGS

- Sad
- Depressed
- "Blue"
- Disappointed
- Lethargic
- Fatigued
- Unmotivated

COMMON BEHAVIORS

- Stay in bed
- Skip class
- Isolate from friends
- Miss work
- Use substances

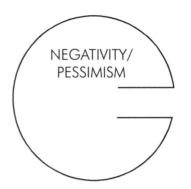

NEGATIVITY/
PESSIMISM

Depression has a biological component and an environmental component. Some people seem to be predisposed to struggle with feelings of low mood more than others. For some, it seems to take a major life catastrophe to affect their mood significantly in any negative way. Others may struggle with at least low-level feelings of depression despite minimal "reason to be depressed." Wherever you fall on this spectrum, identifying triggers is important. Even if you seem to be predisposed to feelings of low mood regularly, identifying triggers can help prevent downward spikes in your already low mood. Again, triggers can be people, places, or things, and some times they are more obvious than at other times. Take a few minutes to answer the following questions that may give you a window into your triggers for depression.

To me, depression is _____

I seem to feel the most depressed when _____

_____

The last time I noticed feeling this way was _____

Themes of times I feel like I have "the blues" include _____

_____

Things that seem to happen right before I feel this way are _____

_____

My triggers for depression are:

1.

2.

3.

4.

5.

Emotions in the "depression family" have a distinct "feel" to them that makes them distinguishable from other feelings. Feelings consistent with this experience can vary from low-level sadness to intense despair and hopelessness. Also, depression often has an *energy* component to it that emotions don't. For instance the more depressed you are, the more you may be prone to feelings of lethargy, decreased motivation, and a desire not to get out of bed, take a shower, or perform other parts of your regular daily routines. "I just don't feel like doing it" is the mantra of the depressed person. *Refer to your face sheet* (Tool 2 in Chapter 2) to identify what feelings you frequently experience related to stress.

Example

My feelings of depression are:

1. Down

2. Sad

3. Disappointed

4. Despairing

5. Hopeless

My feelings of depression are:

1.

2.

3.

4.

5.

The following questions are designed to help you identify your distorted thoughts specifically related to depression. Remember, these thoughts will often fit in the in the category of discounting the positive.

When _____(trigger; see Tool 1 in this chapter) **happens,**

and I feel _____(feelings; see Tool 2 in this chapter),

what am I usually telling myself?

If I were in a cartoon, what would the bubble above my head be saying?

If there were a tape recorder in my head recording my every thought, what would it be saying when someone pushed "play?"

Example

I felt ...	...because I thought...
Sad	I can't live without her in my life.
Discouraged	They are taking so few people — I'll never get into medical school
Hopeless	There's nothing to live for.

Thoughts/Feelings Awareness Log

I felt ...	...because I thought...

"Autopilot" unhealthy coping skills often used to cope with depression can vary from person to person. Some people simply surrender to these feelings and shut life down. Isolating, not returning phone calls from loved ones, lying around on the couch, calling in sick to work, and not taking care of basic activities of daily living can be manifestations of this coping style. Some people's go-to "skills" include attempts not to have to feel the bad feelings. Smoking pot, immersion in alcohol, promiscuous sex, gambling, or other "instant gratification" activities are common methods of attempting to not feel dark feelings. Spend a few minutes trying to identify unhealthy behavior habits you may have developed in response to these feelings.

The last time I felt depressed, I _____

Other things I have done in the past in an attempt to cope when feeling down that that

have in some way hurt me are _____

_____

_____

_____

_____

Some of my "go-to"/"autopilot" depression coping skills are:

1.

2.

3.

4.

5.

As Tool 4 touched upon, things that worked in the past don't always work in the present, and things that work in the present in the short-term don't always work in the long term. In an attempt to increase your awareness, try to identify some of the consequences of your unsuccessful attempted solutions to depression in the past.

Example

Autopilot Coping Skill (from Tool 4)	Current or Past Negative Consequences
Stay in bed all day	Expelled from college
Not answer phone calls	Lost many good friends

Awareness of Consequences Log

Autopilot Coping Skill (from Tool 4)	Current or Past Negative Consequences

Some things I will try the next time I feel depressed are:

1.

2.

3.

4.

5.

6.

7.

8.

9.

10.

Challenging distorted thoughts doesn't always make them go away, but it can put up enough of a "fight" that feelings aren't quite so intense, and it may be at least slightly easier to use some of the skills you identified in Tool 6. Utilize the following *thought log* to attempt to challenge or generate some more *rational responses* to your distorted thoughts you identified in Tool 3. Remember, because depression is often maintained by distinctly *negative* thinking, rational responses to this type of distorted thinking often include attempting to shift thinking more toward the positive.

Example

Distorted Thought	Rational Response
I can't live without her in my life.	I will miss her in my life, so its OK to feel some sadness, but she is better off now, and I can develop other meaningful relationships.
They are taking so few people. I'll never get into medical school.	My grades meet the requirements. I have a good resume. I have a decent chance of getting in. If I don't get in this time, maybe I can later. If I never get in, it's not the end of the world. There are other areas in which I can use my skills and help people medically without being a physician.
There's nothing left to live for.	A lot is going wrong in my life right now, but I still have a mother who cares, my faith in God, and my dog.

Thought Log

Distorted Thought	Rational Response

As a refresher, *core beliefs* are deeply engrained beliefs that serve as filters through which we process information. All of our distorted thinking is the product of one or more harmful beliefs. This technique asks us to take a thought and continue to ask, "What would that mean about me if it were true?" until we get at the core belief at the bottom of the distorted thought. If necessary, refer back to earlier in the chapter to note beliefs that often contribute to stress. Also, remember that many people need a therapist's help to assist with this for a period of time.

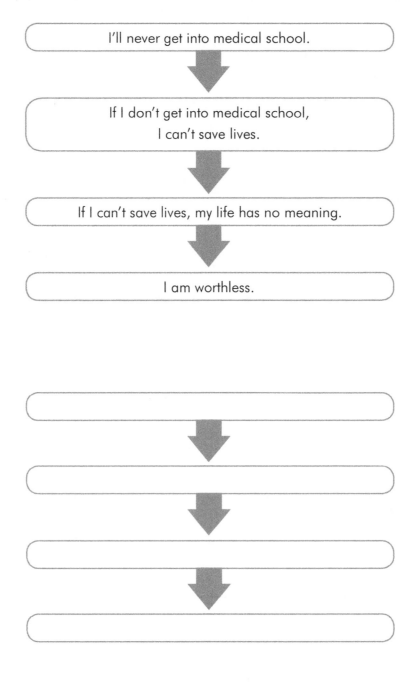

Remember, beliefs come in pairs. For each unhealthy belief you identified, formulate in your own words what the exact opposite of that would mean to you. Flexible language remains important.

Example

My Beliefs

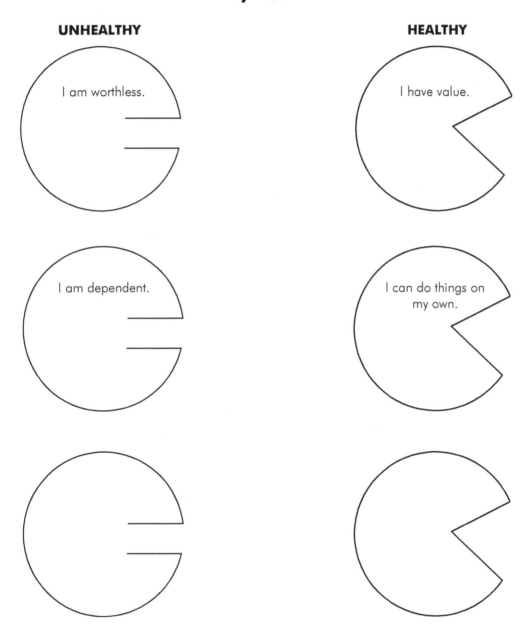

UNHEALTHY

HEALTHY

I am worthless.

I have value.

I am dependent.

I can do things on my own.

The strength of our beliefs significantly influences how often we feel stressful emotions and how strongly we experience them. Take a few minutes and try to assign a strength to each healthy and unhealthy belief. Usually, the easiest way is to use percentages so the total for unhealthy and healthy beliefs equals 100 percent.

Example

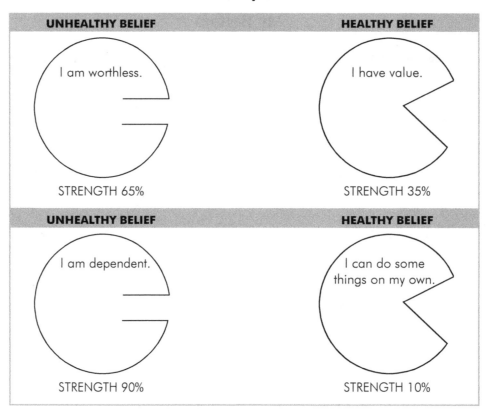

UNHEALTHY BELIEF	HEALTHY BELIEF
I am worthless.	I have value.
STRENGTH 65%	STRENGTH 35%
I am dependent.	I can do some things on my own.
STRENGTH 90%	STRENGTH 10%

Rating the Strength of My Beliefs

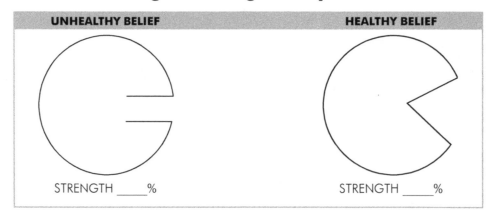

UNHEALTHY BELIEF	HEALTHY BELIEF
STRENGTH _____%	STRENGTH _____%

The following questions may be helpful in reflecting back on different periods of life to uncover some of the experiences you counted as evidence to support your belief (legs to hold up your table). You may need assistance from your therapist to get the most out of this tool.

The first time I ever remember feeling _____[belief]

was _____

The people in my life who influenced me to feel that way were:

Family members _____

_____

Friends/Peers _____

_____

Other significant people _____

_____

Experiences during my elementary school years _____

_____

_____

Experiences during my junior high years _____

_____

_____

Experiences during my high school years _____

_____

_____

Experiences during my college/young adult years _____

_____

_____

Significant experiences since then _____

_____

_____

Use the exercise on the previous page to try to insert some of the "evidence" from your past that you have "counted" to support each belief.

Example

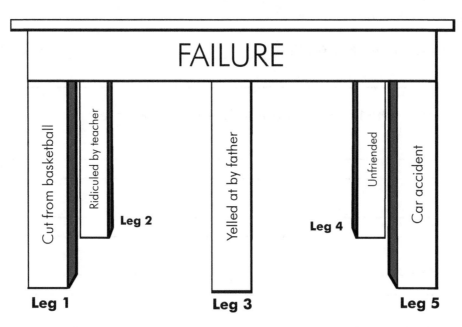

Evidence that I am a failure:

Leg 1: Cut from 8th grade basketball team

Leg 2: Ridiculed for science project by teacher

Leg 3: Father yelled at me in garage for mistake on construction project

Leg 4: Was unfriended by classmate

Leg 5: Got into car accident while texting and driving

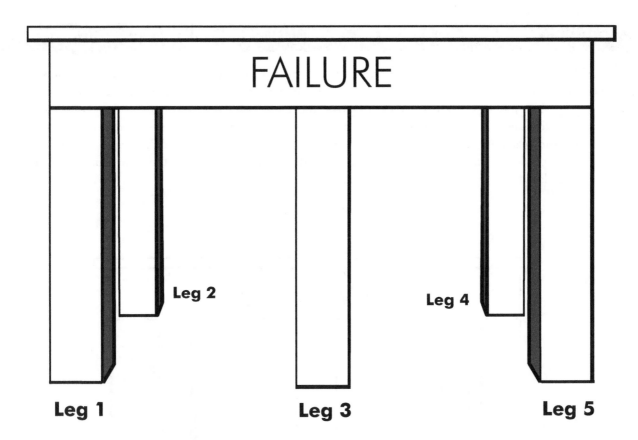

FAILURE

Leg 1

Leg 2

Leg 3

Leg 4

Leg 5

Evidence that I am a failure:

Leg 1:

Leg 2:

Leg 3:

Leg 4:

Leg 5:

Because of how our filters are set up, we often notice instances that support unhealthy beliefs more than we notice experiences that may support our opposite, healthy beliefs. But almost always that "evidence" exists as well. One valuable tool involves forcing ourselves to look back over those very same periods of life purposefully looking to see the evidence that supports our healthy beliefs. Many people often use family members or friends who were around them during each period of life to help them "notice" such evidence. Even if they share things they see as "counting" that you don't think "should count" write them down anyway—you can then use your "add a but" tool to help with that later!

Example

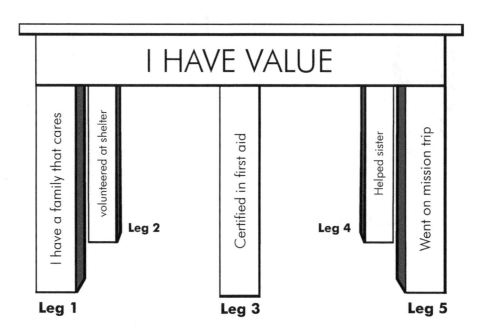

Evidence That I Have Value:

Leg 1: I have family that cares about me.

Leg 2: I volunteered at the animal shelter.

Leg 3: I am certified in first aid.

Leg 4: I helped my sister get out of a bad situation.

Leg 5: I went on a mission trip and helped disaster victims in Haiti.

Healthy Evidence Log

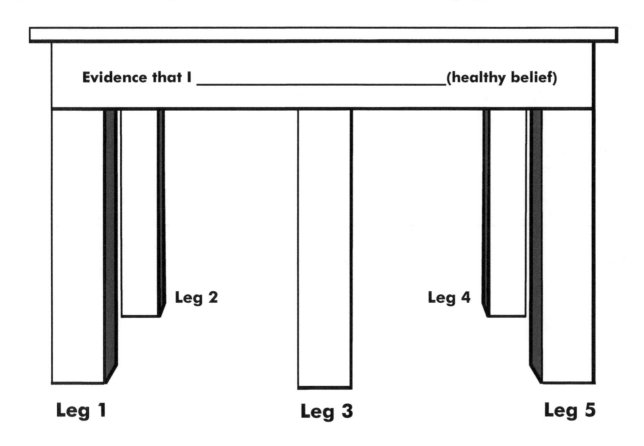

Evidence that I _____(healthy belief)

Leg 1

Leg 2

Leg 3

Leg 4

Leg 5

Leg 1:

Leg 2:

Leg 3:

Leg 4:

Leg 5:

Beliefs *mean* different things to different people. Refer to Tool 13 in Chapter 2 for examples of what it might mean to *have value*. Using that as a guide, compile a list of a few things that support your healthy beliefs about yourself.

Example

Belief	**Components**
1. Have value	**1.** Help other people
	2. Meet medical needs
	3. Benefit animals

Belief	**Components**
1.	**1.**
	2.
	3.
2.	**1.**
	2.
	3.
3.	**1.**
	2.
	3.

Purposefully pay attention to things in life that might count as evidence that your healthy belief could be true.

Example

Evidence that I have value

Date	Evidence
11/10	Passed advanced CPR
11/15	Helped my mom
11/19	Donated to Humane Society
11/24	Volunteered at soup kitchen preparing for Thanksgiving

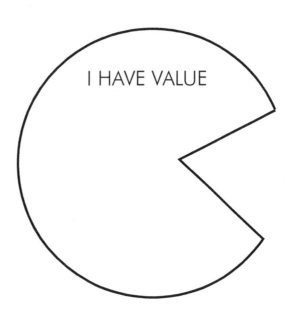

I HAVE VALUE

Evidence that I can be _____ (healthy belief) log

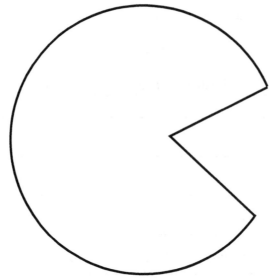

Date	Evidence

One of the toughest things about combating depression is that the things we need to do to get better are the very things we don't feel like doing. Many people stay depressed needlessly for lengthy periods of time because they say things like, "I'll do more when I feel like it," but depression keeps them from ever feeling like it. So as long as we allow our feelings to dictate our behavior (or lack thereof), we stay stuck in a rut.

Thus, one of the tough steps necessary for chipping into depressed feelings is to *do something even though you don't feel like it*. While it sounds a little clichéd, Nike's old slogan, "Just do it" is applicable here. Research has shown that chemical changes occur in our brain as a result of *doing* things that get us "up and moving." A term you may hear in cognitive behavioral therapy to refer to this is *behavioral activation*—activating yourself despite how you feel.

There are a number of ways to facilitate behavioral activation. Two helpful tools are known as *activity monitoring* and *activity scheduling*. Activity monitoring involves paying attention, in very specific detail, to how we are spending our time. Sometimes we can then draw some conclusions regarding how we could restructure our time to be more helpful. Activity scheduling involves purposefully scheduling certain skills or behaviors or activities for certain times of the day. Scheduling can be a powerful way for helping activate our behaviors.

Activity Monitoring Log

Time	Activity (Be Specific)
11:00 am	Got out of bed
11:30 am	Ate two frozen burritos
12:00 pm	Watched TV, went on Facebook
3:00 pm	Went to store
4:00 pm	Took nap
5:30 pm	Played video games
8:30 pm	Ate chips and dip
9:00 pm	Ran on treadmill for 2 hours
11:00 pm	Lay in bed for an hour, couldn't sleep
12:00 am	Watched TV in bed
1:30 am	Eventually fell asleep

Observations

1. Didn't realize how much time I spent playing video games/on Facebook/watching TV

2. Didn't think about getting on treadmill so late and how might affect my sleep

3. Lay in bed too long when I couldn't sleep

4. Have stopped eating healthy breakfasts

5. Managed to go through whole day without talking to another human being live or on the phone

Small changes I am willing to make include:

1. Begin bedtime routine involving shower, sleeping pills, and light music

2. Go shopping for healthy breakfast foods/Make attempt to eat healthy breakfast every day

3. Move treadmill time to morning

4. Try to call or meet one person each day for at least 15 min

Activity Monitoring Log

Time	Activity (Be Specific)
6:00 am	
7:00 am	
8:00 am	
9:00 am	
10:00 am	
11:00 am	
12:00 pm	
1:00 pm	
2:00 pm	
3:00 pm	
4:00 pm	
5:00 pm	
6:00 pm	
7:00 pm	
8:00 pm	
9:00 pm	
10:00 pm	
11:00 pm	
12:00 am	
1:00 am	
2:00 am	
3:00 am	
4:00 am	
5:00 am	

Observations:

1.

2.

3.

Small changes that I am willing to make include:

1.

2.

3.

Activity Scheduling

Now try to be purposeful about what kinds of things you do during your day. Plan some things that you want to be sure to accomplish that day, and make the times mean something. Pretend you have an appointment with yourself at each time to do each scheduled event. There are different versions of this tool. This particular version asks you to plan your day in advance and record what you planned. It also has an empty space where you can record how well you did with following through and actually doing what you planned!

Research has shown three areas of coping to be especially helpful for people who struggle with depression: *mastery, pleasure,* and *meaning. Mastery* skills are especially important for people who value performance or accomplishment. If you are one of these people, you probably feel better about yourself when get things done. If you are one of these people, chances are you have made a "to-do" list or two in your life! These can be powerful tools for individuals who value performance. If this is you, try making a list of things to accomplish for the day. It is important to make your list significant enough that it "matters" to you so that you are able to give yourself credit for having completed it but also realistic so you have a good chance of actually accomplishing it. Mastery lists can include basic household chores, errands, or daily business, in addition to steps in pursuit of larger life goals.

Choose from the following list or generate your own things you can feel good for having accomplished. And give yourself credit for each thing you accomplish.

Mastery-Related Tasks

1. Thinking I have done a full day's work
2. Cleaning a room in my house
3. Planning for a starting a new career
4. Thinking about ways to advance the career I'm already in
5. Running errands
6. Planning a day's activities
7. Doing laundry
8. Putting on make-up
9. Thinking how it will be when I finish school
10. Mowing the lawn
11. Working on my car
12. Pulling weeds
13. Repairing things around the house
14. Taking care of my plants
15. Buying and selling stocks
16. Losing weight
17. Doing embroidery
18. Cross-stitching
19. Joining a club
20. Painting my nails (and noticing when each of the 20 gets done!)
21. Writing poetry
22. Sewing
23. Going to work
24. Gardening
25. Refinishing furniture
26. Making lists of tasks
27. Going bike riding (give yourself credit for each mile!)
28. Completing a task
29. Thinking about past achievements
30. Planning future achievements
31. Making a grocery list
32. Exchanging emails
33. Photography
34. Voting for candidate I support
35. Solving riddles
36. Knitting
37. Crocheting
38. Quilting
39. Doing crossword puzzles
40. Making jigsaw puzzles
41. Doing school assignment
42. Doing therapy homework
43. Paying bills
44. Picking up around the house
45. Volunteering
46. Playing games online
47. Painting the house
48. Saving money
49. Working on a community service project
50. Playing a game on my smart phone

My Mastery ("To-Do") List for Today

1. Pay bills

2. Do two loads of laundry

3. Complete my application for graduate school

4. Go to the credit union

5. Finish my Sunday school lesson

My Mastery ("To-Do") List for Today

1.

2.

3.

4.

5.

A clinical term you may hear to describe a category of depression symptoms is *anhedonia*, or *anhedonic symptoms*. These refer to a set of symptoms that can include lack of desire or lack of pleasure. Therefore, skills that involve inducing pleasure are vital to incorporate into your activity scheduling on a daily basis. Below are a few examples. You may select pleasurable events from this list or come up with your own.

Pleasure-Related Tasks

1. Soaking in the bathtub
2. Burning incense
3. Kissing
4. Taking a weekend trip
5. Thinking about a past vacation
6. Going on a date/flirting
7. Nurturing your pet
8. Going for a walk or jog
10. Listening to music
11. Going to a party or get-together
12. Being outdoors
13. Looking at photos from past trips
14. Reading
15. Brushing your hair
16. Giving or receiving a hug
17. Remembering beautiful scenery
18. Playing tennis, Frisbee golf or another sport
19. Drawing or looking at someone else's art
20. Catching up with old friends on Facebook
21. Trying a new support group
22. Trying a new church
23. Going to a casino
24. Renting a movie
25. Going to a sporting event
27. Going to the gym

28. Dancing
29. Karate
30. Enjoying nature
31. Yoga
32. Sleeping
33. Getting a massage
34. Going for a drive
35. Calling a supportive person
36. Flying a kite
37. Praying
38. Buying flowers
39. Having a manicure/pedicure
40. Going swimming
41. Watching a sunrise/sunset
42. Riding a bike
43. Having responsible sex
44. Having a quiet evening at home
45. Drinking a cup of coffee
45. Going to a lake
46. Getting together with old friends
47. Exercising to an aerobics/yoga DVD
48. Going to a play
49. Getting on the Internet and researching something you enjoy
50. Giving a small gift to someone else

My Pleasurable Events

1.

2.

3.

4.

5.

6.

7.

8.

9.

10.

The third area associated with depression has to do with *meaning*. This is different for different people. You may be familiar with the story of Victor Frankl, who survived what could be considered among the worst environmental experiences—a concentration camp. Yet he came out with a positive attitude because of his development of, and focus on, what the meaning of life was for him. For many people, this involves issues related to religion or faith. For others, it may include meaningful relationships, worthy causes, or other meaningful things. The more consistently we live our lives in accordance with our values, or what we consider to be meaningful, the more significance we believe we have, which contributes to our sense of well-being. Identify what gives your life meaning, and be sure to incorporate specific activities that support it in your activity scheduling.

Meaning Worksheet

To me the most meaningful areas of life are:

1. Faith

2. Family

3. Education

Meaningful action steps I will take today include:

1. Attend a service

2. Help my elderly aunt

3. Sing in choir

4. Study for my exam

5. Pray

Meaning Worksheet

To me the most meaningful areas of life are:

1.

2.

3.

Meaningful action steps I will take today include:

1.

2.

3.

4.

5.

Has anyone ever told you, "Just count your blessings—you have so much to be thankful for"? That advice drives many depressed people nuts, because the people who are saying those words typically have *no idea what you are going through*. All human beings need to be validated. Therefore, acknowledging losses, hurts, and needs and having them validated is important. However, the mistake some people struggling with depression make is that they *only* find people who will validate them. Have you ever heard the phrase "misery loves company?" Some depressed people, usually without meaning to, seek people who will validate their pain without challenging them to try to move forward with more positive thinking and behavior.

It feels good to know that the feelings we are experiencing are "valid." However, just because they are valid emotions and it may be completely understandable how we got there, that doesn't mean it's helpful that we stay there. By only seeking validation, many depressed individuals unknowingly develop a "victim mentality," which ultimately fuels their feelings of misery. Because of this, it is important that we be able to express our hurts, wounds, and losses and get validated for them.

It is also important to identify some positives to focus on. The term *silver lining* is often used to describe finding a little bit of good in a bad situation. There may be some situations in which we are not able to find a silver lining—at least at this point. If that is the case, it may take looking outside the particular negative situation that is bringing you down and trying to find some positives, or blessings in *other* areas of life. Perhaps you are not able to find any positives about being robbed yesterday, but it is still to your advantage that you have a family that can help you, that you still have a place to live, and a dog that brings you much joy. So, while it would be dishonest to say, "That robbery was good. I'm glad it happened," it also will not be helpful to your mood if you continue to focus on thoughts such as, "Why do these things always happen to me?"

Thinking about difficult situations in a healthy manner involves both *acknowledging painful situations* and *not dwelling on them*. Don't let that negative filter creep in and keep you from enjoying other aspects of life even if some of what you are going through is terrible. The following tools will help you do just that: acknowledge legitimate painful situations in your life while also coming up with some positives, or blessings in your life as well.

Example

Acknowledgment Log

Painful situations I'm dealing with in life now include:

1. Sister said mean words to me

2. Supervisor criticized me

3. Losses that I'm currently dealing with include: Husband left me

People I can talk to/places I can go to get these validated are:

1. Grief recovery support group

2. My Rabbi

3. My coworker, who has dealt with my boss longer than I have

My Acknowledgment Log

Painful situations I'm dealing with in life now include:

Losses I'm currently dealing with include:

People I can talk to/places I can go to get these validated are:

1.

2.

3.

Example

Count Your Blessings
(Things I Have to Be Thankful for Even Though Parts of My Life Are Hard Right Now)

1. My sister

2. My nieces

3. My dogs

4. My aunt

5. My support group

6. Knitting

7. Going to the movies

8. Roses

9. The color red

10. The fact that it's a nice day today

Count Your Blessings
(Things I Have to Be Thankful for Even Though Parts of My Life Are Hard Right Now)

1.

2.

3.

4.

5.

6.

7.

8.

9.

10.

Now, to help you with those "in the moment" reactions, refer to Tool 20 in Chapter 2 to develop your cards. Remember, the coping card gives you alternative things to *do* "in the moment." Cue cards help you with how to *think*.

Example

When I feel _____*depressed*_____ (behavior from Tool 4),

I can (choices from Tool 6):

1. *Get out of bed* _____

2. *Take a shower/get dressed* _____

3. *Call my aunt* _____

Your Coping Card

When I feel _____ (behavior from Tool 4),

I can (choices from Tool 6):

1. _____

2. _____

3. _____

Example

Cognitive Cue Card

Just because _I didn't get into medical_ **doesn't mean** _I'm worthless. I could still_
school

be a nurse or a physician's assistant or just keep working as an EMT.

I know _the role in which I help people_ **is true because** _people appreciate being_
is not important

helped regardless of what my title is. I have value as a healer everytime I help people.

Your Cognitive Cue Card

Cognitive Cue Card

Just because _____ **doesn't mean** _____

_____

I know _____ **is true because** _____

_____

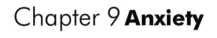

Chapter 9 **Anxiety**

COMMON BELIEFS
- Helpless
- Vulnerable
- Approval Seeking/Unlovable
- Failure

COMMON DISTORTIONS
- Fortune-telling
- Mind-reading
- Magnification

COMMON AUTOMATIC THOUGHTS
- "I can't cope with this."
- "It is unacceptable to not be liked."
- "The world is dangerous."
- "People are untrustworthy."
- "I could get hurt."
- "What if I can't do it?"

COMMON FEELINGS
- Anxious
- Worried
- Fearful
- Scared
- Afraid
- Panicked

COMMON BEHAVIORS
- Avoid
- Isolate
- Shut down

Some people are more anxious than others, and different people worry about different things. Later in this chapter, a tool that will help you assess more specifically how anxiety impacts you is presented. For now, similarly to how you have done with previous emotions and symptom sets, try to identify your general triggers for anxiety. Again, *triggers* can be people, places, or things and some are more obvious than others. Take a few minutes to answer the following questions that may give you a window into your triggers for anxiety.

To me, anxiety is _____

I feel the most anxious when _____

The last time I noticed feeling this way was _____

Themes of times I feel anxious include _____

Things that seem to happen right before I feel this way are _____

_____

My triggers for anxiety are:

1.

2.

3.

4.

5.

Feelings of anxiety may be similar to feelings related to stress but are vastly different from the other feelings or symptom sets discussed in this tools manual. Feelings in the "anxiety family" may include but are not limited to *anxiety, fear, worry, fright, being scared, being startled, feeling claustrophobic, being overwhelmed,* and *panic.* Refer to your "Feelings Face Sheet" (Tool 2 in Chapter 2) to identify what feelings related to anxiety you frequently experience.

My anxiety-related feelings are:

1.

2.

3.

4.

5.

The following questions are designed to help you identify your distorted thoughts specifically related to anxiety. Remember, these thoughts will often fit in the categories of fortune telling, mind reading, and magnification statements.

When _____(trigger; see Tool 1 in this chapter) **happens,**

and I feel _____(feelings; see Tool 2 in this chapter),

what am I usually telling myself?

If I were in a cartoon, what would the bubble above my head be saying?

If there were a tape recorder in my head recording my every thought, what would it be saying when someone pushed "play?"

Example

I felt ...	...because I thought...
Anxious	She will probably say no.
Worried	I'm afraid she may wreck my car. She's never driven a standard shift before.
Panic	The last time I was alone with a man, he abused me. I am in grave danger again.

Thoughts/Feelings Awareness Log

I felt ...	...because I thought...

There is clearly one "go-to" coping skill that is the most common for people who struggle with anxiety. It is *avoidance*. Many people choose skills designed to avoid triggers that induce anxiety. An example of this would be a boy never asking a girl out on a date for fear she might say no. By never asking, he does prevent anxiety related to rejection but also never gets to find out if he could get a date and stays lonely until he is willing to take that risk. Spend a few minutes and consider what you typically do when you feel anxious.

The last time I felt really anxious I _____

Other things I have done in the past in an attempt to cope with anxiety are _____

_____

_____

_____

_____

One situation I remember avoiding as a result of feeling anxious was _____

_____

_____

My "go-to"/"autopilot" "go-to"/"autopilot" anxiety management coping skills are:

1.

2.

3.

4.

5.

As Tool 4 touched on, things that worked in the past don't always work in the present, and things that work in the present in the short term don't always work in the long term. In attempt to increase your awareness, try to identify some of the consequences of your unsuccessful attempts to cope with anxiety in the past.

Example

Autopilot Coping Skill (from Tool 4)	Current or Past Negative Consequences
"Chickened out" of interview	Lost out on potentially good job, trouble paying bills now
Didn't go out on a date with Jerry	Missed out on a good guy. Now I have to watch Jennifer date him.
Didn't check mail for 2 months	My paycheck is being garnished

Awareness of Consequences Log

Autopilot Coping Skill (from Tool 4)	Current or Past Negative Consequences

Some things I will try the next time I feel anxious are:

1.

2.

3.

4.

5.

6.

7.

8.

9.

10.

Challenging distorted thoughts doesn't always make them go away but can put up enough of a "fight" that feelings aren't quite so intense, and it may be at least slightly easier to use some of the skills you identified in Tool 6. Utilize the following *thought log* to attempt to challenge or generate some more *rational responses* to the distorted thoughts you identified in Tool 3. Remember, since anxiety is always a product of those "what ifs?" remember to be on guard for fortune telling, mind reading, and magnification thoughts, and remember to challenge then with probes to assess the actual risk and remind yourself of your actual abilities.

Example

Distorted Thought	Rational Response
She will probably say no.	I won't know until I ask. Even though it's been 2 years since I asked a girl out, the last one said yes. If she says no, I'll be right where I am now. I have nothing to lose.
I'm afraid she may wreck my car. She's never driven a standard shift before.	I have to let her try if she's ever going to learn. The car is insured. She's only going six blocks and will be driving slowly, so even if she struggles it is highly likely she'll be fine.
The last time I was alone with a man, he abused me . I am in grave danger again.	Most men aren't abusive. I've been with him often in groups, and he seems gentle. Even though I am alone with him, I am in the theatre, so I'm really not alone. He has been nothing but nice to me. If I'm going to start dating again I have to start somewhere, and he seems like the safest bet I've encountered in a long time.

Thought Log

Distorted Thought	Rational Response

As a refresher, *core beliefs* are deeply engrained beliefs that serve as filters through which we process information. All of our distorted thinking is the product of one or more harmful beliefs. This technique asks us to take a thought and continue to ask, "What would that mean about us if it were true?" until we get to the core belief at the bottom of the distorted thought. If necessary, refer back to earlier in the chapter to note beliefs that often contribute to stress. Also, remember many people need a therapist's help to assist with this for a period of time.

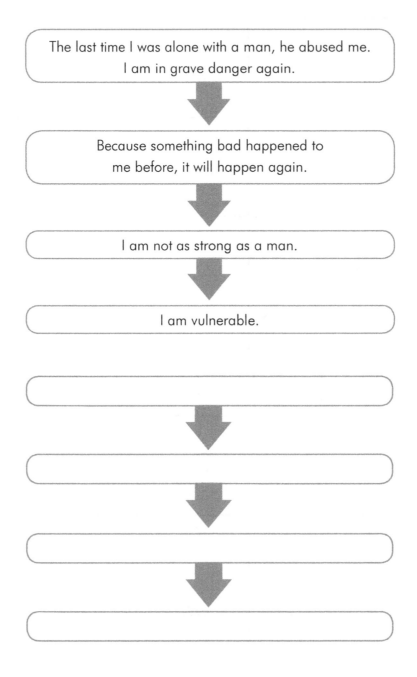

Remember, beliefs come in pairs. For each unhealthy belief you identified, formulate in your words what the exact opposite of that would mean to you. Flexible language remains important.

Example

My Beliefs

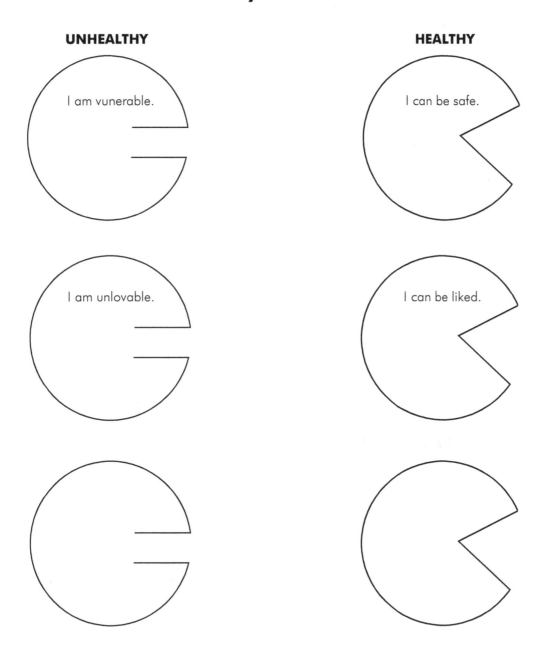

UNHEALTHY

HEALTHY

I am vunerable.

I can be safe.

I am unlovable.

I can be liked.

The strength of our beliefs significantly influences how often we feel anxiety related emotions and how strongly we experience them. Take a few minutes and try to assign strengths to each healthy and unhealthy belief. The easiest way is usually to use percentages so the total for unhealthy and healthy beliefs equals 100 percent.

Example

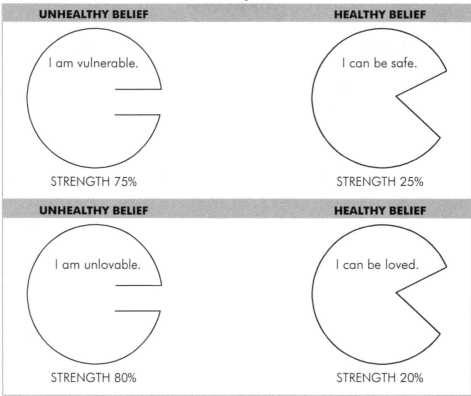

Rating the Strength of My Beliefs

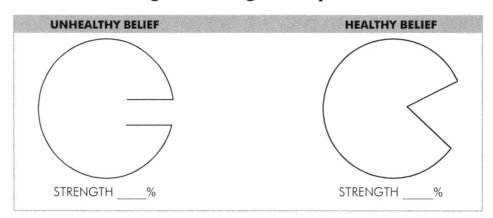

The following questions may be helpful in reflecting back on different periods of life to uncover some of the experiences you counted as evidence to support your belief (legs to hold up your table). You may need assistance from your therapist to get the most out of this tool.

The first time I ever remember feeling _____[belief]

was _____

The people in my life who influenced me to feel that way were:

Family members _____

_____

Friends/Peers _____

_____

Other significant people _____

_____

Experiences during my elementary school years _____

_____

_____

Experiences during my junior high years _____

_____

_____

Experiences during my high school years _____

_____

_____

Experiences during my college/young adult years _____

_____

_____

Significant experiences since then _____

_____

_____

Use the exercise on the previous page to try to insert some of the "evidence" from your past that you have "counted" to support each belief:

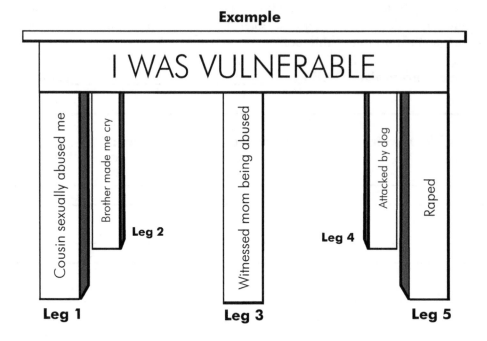

Example

I WAS VULNERABLE

Cousin sexually abused me — Leg 1

Brother made me cry — Leg 2

Witnessed mom being abused — Leg 3

Attacked by dog — Leg 4

Raped — Leg 5

Evidence that I was vulnerable:

Leg 1: Cousin sexually abused me at age 8.

Leg 2: Brother would hold me down and hold frog over me until I cried.

Leg 3: Witnessed my mom being physically abused by boyfriend.

Leg 4: Attacked by dog as a teenager—was hurt badly and had to be hospitalized.

Leg 5: Raped 3 years ago by man in my support group.

Unhealthy Evidence Log

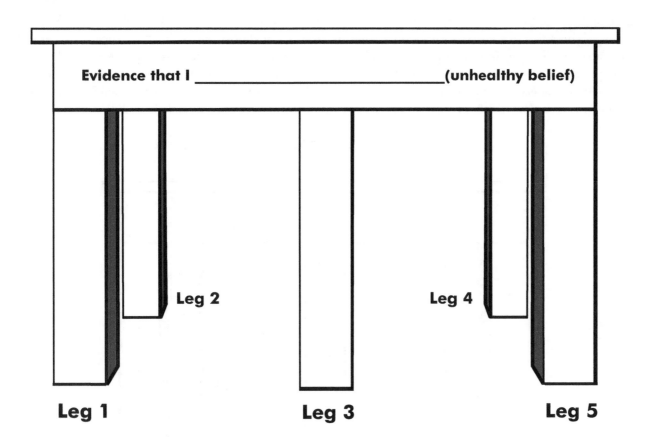

Evidence that I _____(unhealthy belief)

Leg 1

Leg 2

Leg 3

Leg 4

Leg 5

Leg 1:

Leg 2:

Leg 3:

Leg 4:

Leg 5:

Because of how our filters are set up, we often notice instances that support the unhealthy beliefs more than we notice experiences that may support our opposite, healthy beliefs, but almost always that "evidence" exists as well. One valuable tool involves forcing ourselves to look back over those very same periods of life purposefully looking to see the evidence that supports our healthy beliefs. Many people often use family members or friends who were around them during each period of life to help them "notice" such evidence. Even if they share things they see as "counting" that you don't think "should count" write them down anyway— a tool to help with that is provided later!

Example

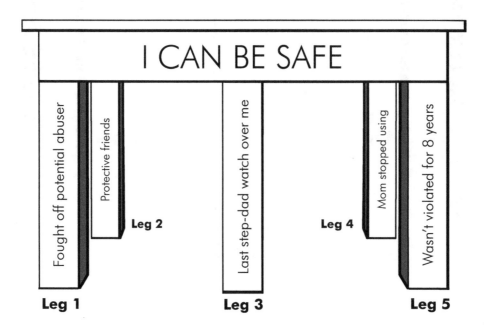

Evidence that I can be safe:

Leg 1: When I was 14, I fought off a potential abuser.

Leg 2: I had many friends who helped protect me .

Leg 3: My third step-dad watched over me.

Leg 4: Once my mom stopped using drugs, we lived in a safer neighborhood.

Leg 5: From age 14 to 22 I wasn't violated in any way

Healthy Evidence Log

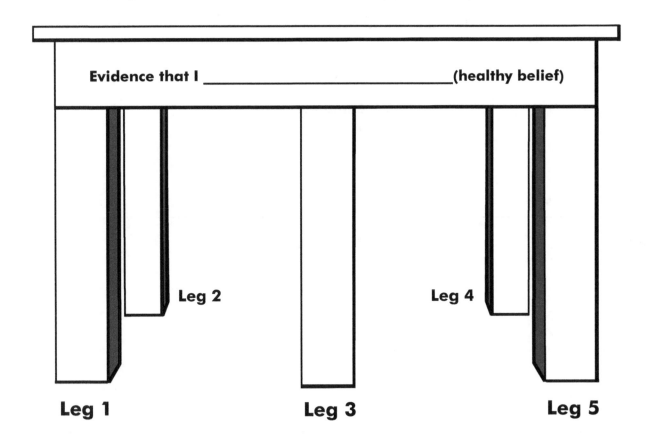

Evidence that I _____(healthy belief)

Leg 1

Leg 2

Leg 3

Leg 4

Leg 5

Leg 1:

Leg 2:

Leg 3:

Leg 4:

Leg 5:

Beliefs *mean* different things to different people. Refer to Tool 13 in Chapter 2 for examples of what it might mean to *have value*. Using that as a guide, compile a list of a few things that support your healthy beliefs about yourself.

Example

Belief	**Components**
1. I can be safe	**1.** Physically safe
	2. Emotionally safe
	3. Safe in relationships

Belief	**Components**
1.	**1.**
	2.
	3.
2.	**1.**
	2.
	3.
3.	**1.**
	2.
	3.

Purposefully pay attention to things in life that might count as evidence that your healthy belief could be true.

Example

Evidence that I can be safe

Date	Evidence
9/10	Spent 2 hours in crowded mall—felt claustrophobic, but nothing happened
9/16	Stayed out past midnight—was with safe people and was fine
9/20	Went with group of people to scary part of town, but we made good choices, so I didn't have to miss the theme park as I did last time
9/23	Went out on a date, and Jeff treated me well
9/24	Dad gave me a hug and told me he would always be there for me—even though I am now an adult and not supposed to need that—I felt safe like when I was a little girl

I CAN BE SAFE

Evidence that I can be _____ (healthy belief) log

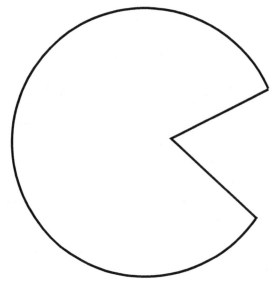

Date	Evidence

A friend of mine once rushed into a meeting 10 minutes late and jokingly asked, "Has anyone seen my time? I think I've lost it!" Many people live life on overdrive. Overbooked. Overscheduled. Always rushed. Burned out. This sense of urgency robs us of our peace in life and keeps us from enjoying the moment. The demands of Western society have made it increasingly difficult for us to live life with any *margin*. Many are surprised to discover they have actually been unknowingly contributing their anxiety by their inability to take control of their time. The good news is that *we control how we spend our time!* Creating additional time in our lives may mean making some difficult choices, but the choice really is up to us. If we are willing to make different choices, we can significantly reduce our anxiety by learning to manage our time.

Some tips for taking control of your time include:

- Examine your priorities—be honest with yourself about what is really important in your life.

- Develop a plan based on those priorities—devote time only to those things that you deem the most valuable.

- Create *margin*—leave time for unforeseen events, traffic, things out of your control.

- Say no to things that are lower on your priority list—it is possible to be involved in too many noble causes. Only commit to things you have time for at that point in your life and work to get better at telling people no.

Steps I will take to take control of my time:

1.

2.

3.

4.

5.

Avoidant behaviors are the most common types of behaviors used by individuals who struggle with anxiety. Anxiety is developed and perpetuated by believing something is more threatening than it really is and by minimizing our ability to cope with that perceived or actual threat. Many people who struggle with anxiety have experienced actual danger in their lives. Many have been hurt physically or emotionally. But not all people who have been hurt struggle with anxiety. Anxiety persists when we continue to view threats as currently present even when in reality they may not be. It is common then for people to cope by using what are called *safety behaviors*.

Safety behaviors are any behaviors that decrease anxiety in the short term (so the person feels "safe") but in actuality make the anxiety worse in the long term. There is a good chance that some of the "autopilot" coping skills you identified in Tool 4 may fit into this category. One of the most important steps for overcoming anxiety is identifying and eliminating safety behaviors. Many say, "If I give up my safety net, I'll become more anxious." Why would a chapter devoted to helping alleviate anxiety ask you to do stop doing things that make you less anxious? The only way to truly help your anxiety get better in the long run is to retrain your brain to recognize that things you once thought were dangerous are not and that you are generally safer than you previously believed—or that the actual threat isn't nearly as great as you previously thought. The reality is that 90 percent of the things we worry about never happen. Safety behaviors block the brain from learning this crucial lesson.

Most people are not aware that safety behaviors are harmful, and many do not even recognize they are doing them. Therefore, identifying your safety behaviors is an important first step. Take a few minutes and consider behaviors you may be doing that help you feel less anxious immediately but that may be keeping you from being able to test your fear-based beliefs.

Example
Safety Behaviors

- Taking stairs instead of elevators
- Taking a drink before every social event to "loosen up"
- Driving instead of flying
- Checking the door 10 times before going to bed every night
- Going to early church service because "hardly anyone else is there"
- Shopping at 2 am
- Taking driving route that takes 30 extra minutes so as not to have to cross a bridge
- Not initiating conversation
- Never going shopping for fear of overspending
- Changing the subject when asked about something uncomfortable

Dr. Martin Antony's *The Anti-Anxiety Handbook* lists some safety behaviors common with specific conditions you might want to consider when compiling your list of safety behaviors. This book is an excellent resource if anxiety is exclusively what you struggle with.

Anxiety Problem or Diagnosis	Common Safety Behaviors
Panic disorder and agoraphobia	• Sitting in aisle seat in theatre to facilitate quick escape • Always having a "safe" person around when going to feared situations • Frequently checking pulse to ensure heart rate is not racing • Sitting down and resting when panic begins
Social anxiety and shyness	• Wearing make-up to hide blushing • Wearing light clothing to hide sweating in public • Over-preparing for presentations • Avoiding eye contact when talking to others
Generalized anxiety and worry	• Leaving home extra early for appointments so there is no chance of being late • Phoning children frequently to make sure they are OK • Not buying things you can easily afford for fear someday you may have no money
Obsessive-compulsive issues	• Wearing gloves when touching things that may be "contaminated" • Excessive hand washing • Repeated checking to make sure work done correctly
Anxiety from past trauma	• Carrying pepper spray to protect yourself from possible assault • Driving extra slowly to avoid car accident • Walking with your back to the wall in public to prevent being attacked
Phobias related to blood and needles	• Lying down during blood test to avoid becoming faint • Looking away during blood draw
Phobias related to animals	• Checking for dogs through window before going for a walk • Carrying umbrella to protect self from harmless snakes
Other specific phobias	• Flying business class to avoid feeling closed in • Driving only in right lane to make it easy to pull over if necessary • Over-preparing for tests or exams

My Safety Behaviors

1.

2.

3.

4.

5.

6.

7.

8.

9.

10.

In 1999, David Satcher, then U. S. surgeon general, wrote perhaps the most complete review of mental health and treatment ever published. In it he stated that the most important and critical part of treatment for anxiety is "exposure to stimuli"; in other words, facing your fears. You may have heard the term *exposure*. Exposure is probably the most important strategy for recovery. Unfortunately, it can also be the most difficult because it requires you to do the things you fear the most. This obviously involves being willing to gradually work to reduce the safety behaviors you identified in Tool 16. It's one thing to *tell* yourself something isn't as scary as you thought it was. It's another thing to *prove* it to yourself. Exposure-based strategies are based on the principle that we all get used to things over time.

Although extremely effective when done right, exposure therapy can often be harmful if not done properly, so it is best that you plan this series of exercises with your therapist. As you plan to face your fears, remember one thing: The goal is not to do the exercise without experiencing any anxiety. The goal is to test your belief to see if your fearful perceptions are true. If they aren't true and as you *experience* this over time, your brain learns to process threat differently and your anxiety will decrease. Anxiety typically decreases with gradual exposure over time, so be patient. Occasionally (but rarely), catastrophic beliefs do turn out to be true. If this is the case, do not fear! The tool discussed next will help you cope with this situation.

Another helpful tool from *The Anti-Anxiety Handbook* to help you work with exposure is the following exposure log (pp 157–159, with permission).

Example

Exposure Log

Date	Belief	Pre-test (%)	Test	Result	Post-test (%)
6/13	Bridge will collapse if I go over it	95	Visualize driving over bridge	Made it safely, bridge didn't collapse	90
6/15		90	Watch other cars drive over bridge	55 cars crossed safely in 1 hour, none fell through	80
6/17		80	Drove over bridge myself first time	Made it safely, bridge didn't collapse	60

My Exposure Log

Date	Belief	Pre-test (%)	Test	Result	Post-test (%)

We said earlier in this book that 90 percent of the things we worry about never happen. In these cases, the goal is to retrain our brain to be able to assess the threat accurately so we don't feel fearful when there is no real, current threat. But, what about those few times we are right and something really is dangerous? The same survey that taught us that 90 percent of the things we worry about never happen also showed us that, even when they do, 79 percent of the time people said, "I handled it better than I thought I would." So even when there is a clear and present danger, we often sell ourselves short when it comes to our ability to cope. Often, we really do have the resources at our disposal to handle the anxiety-provoking event. Resources can be internal or external. Examples of internal resources may include coping skills, personal strengths, and personality traits. External resources may include significant others, medications, and support groups. Tool 18 asks you consider the resources you have to cope with life's anxiety-provoking situations.

Example

My Resources

1. Rational thinking skills

2. Meditation

3. Faith in God

4. My support group

5. My mother

6. I am a good problem solver

7. I am resilient

8. I am a fighter

9. I have a positive attitude

10. I can go to my safe place

My Resources

1.

2.

3.

4.

5.

6.

7.

8.

9.

10.

One surefire way to stay anxious is to continue to insist on knowing things *for sure*. The reality is that there are few things in this life that we can know for certain, and when it comes to the future, we can guarantee virtually nothing! Regardless, millions of people drive themselves crazy with thoughts like

- "I must know."
- "How could it be?"
- "I just can't go on until I know why?"
- "I have to have an answer."
- "I just need to know for sure."

Many people prone to worry think the same thoughts over and over and over and over. You may hear this referred to as *unproductive worry*. Some professionals may use a fancy term, *ruminate*. I had a patient who said, "I used to be like a cow chewing on his cud." Another patient who lived on a farm said, "I'm kind of like that pig who 'wallers' in the mud." Animal comparisons aside, the better we can get at tolerating uncertainty, the less anxious we will feel. Some skills for learning to tolerate uncertainty include

- Acceptance
- Examining pros and cons of worry
- Listing things you have endured in life that were worse than uncertainty
- Prayer/meditation
- Improving the moment
- Perspective exercises
- Doing a Google search on "suffer"/"suffering" and then rating your discomfort
- Looking for meaning in discomfort
- Searching for "silver lining"

Rational responses helpful for tolerating uncertainty include

- Asking "is there anything I can do?"—If so, do it! If not let it go"
- "Worrying will only hurt"
- "Let go and let God"
- "Someday I may know, but its OK not to now"
- "I don't have to know"
- "I can have faith that it will turn out OK…and if it doesn't, I have resources to cope."
- "Uncertainty is uncomfortable, but it's not intolerable"

My skills for tolerating uncertainty

1.

2.

3.

4.

5.

6.

7.

8.

9.

10.

Now, to help you with those "heat of the moment" reactions, refer to Tool 20 in Chapter 2 to develop your cards. Remember, the coping card gives you alternative things to *do* "in the moment." Cue cards help you with how to *think*.

Example

When I feel _____*anxious*_____ (behavior from Tool 4),

I can (choices from Tool 6):

1. Ask myself, "What's the worst thing that could happen?"

2. Call a member of my support team.

3. Take a small risk.

Your Coping Card

When I feel _____ (behavior from Tool 4),

I can (choices from Tool 6):

1. _____

2. _____

3. _____

Example

Cognitive Cue Card

Just because _I feel vulnerable_ **doesn't mean** _I am. I was legitimately in_

danger when I was with Ron, but Kennon is nothing like him.

I know _he is a good guy_ **is true because** _I have been with him_

several times recently, and he has only been gentle. I am safe with him.

Your Cognitive Cue Card

Cognitive Cue Card

Just because _____ **doesn't mean** _____

_____

I know _____ **is true because** _____

_____

Chapter 10 **Anger**

COMMON BELIEFS

- Powerless (diminished)
- Others are incompetent
- Entitlement
- Punitive

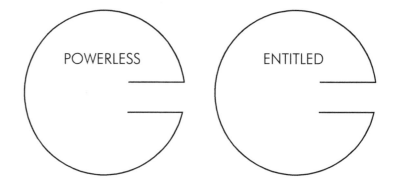

COMMON DISTORTIONS

- Should statements (others)
- Personalization
- Rationalization

COMMON AUTOMATIC THOUGHTS

- "He should do what I ask!"
- "She shouldn't do that!"
- "It isn't right!"
- "How dare they disrespect me!"
- "Its OK to yell/scream/hit because he deserved it."

COMMON FEELINGS

- Mad
- Irritated
- Frustrated
- Annoyed
- Enraged

COMMON BEHAVIORS

- Yelling
- Screaming
- Using profanity
- Destruction of property
- Verbal, physical abuse

Unlike depression and, to a lesser extent, anxiety (which many people experience on some level on a regular and ongoing basis), anger is an emotion experienced more *situationally*. Because of this, identification of triggers is more important with anger than with many other emotions (because there always is a trigger). Perhaps you have heard the expressions "he is mad at the world" or "she has a chip on her shoulder." Some people do seem more chronically annoyed, but whether those people are aware of them or not, there are always reasons. There are always earlier events in a person's life that have contributed to their viewing life in a manner that predisposes them to irritability, and there are always activating triggers in the present. Keep in mind that anger is always related to our values, or the things that are important to us. One helpful exercise involves paying close attention to what life events trigger these feelings, specifically focusing on when others violate our values. Again, triggers can be people, places, or things. Take a few minutes to answer the following questions that may give you a window into your anger-related triggers.

I usually notice my anger most when _____

The last time I got enraged was _____

The last time I got annoyed was _____

The person or people most likely to make me mad are _____

_____

One issue I feel strongly about that always makes me mad is _____

The last time I felt wronged and got "ticked off" was _____

My anger triggers are:

1.

2.

3.

4.

5.

Anger is an emotion that is difficult for some people to express. Some people grew up in families where anger was associated with fear. Many people have internalized ideas, like "anger is always bad" or "anger always leads to violence." For others, anger is the only emotion they know—or at least the only emotion that is acceptable to express. It is common for people who grew up in families where sharing emotions was a sign of weakness to have developed that "tough guy" or "tough girl" front. For these individuals, expressing other emotions is a sign of vulnerability they aren't willing to reveal. Anger takes many forms and can be felt or experienced to varying degrees. Anger is a normal human emotion. Everyone feels it in some form. Review your "Feelings Face Sheet" from Tool 2 in Chapter 2 and identify feelings in the "anger family." These might range from mildly annoyed to extremely enraged.

My anger feelings are:

1.

2.

3.

4.

5.

The following questions are designed to help you identify your distorted thoughts specifically related to anger. Remember, these thoughts will often fit in the category of "shoulding others" and occur in response to one of our values being violated.

When _____(trigger; see Tool 1 in this chapter) **happens,**

and I feel _____(feelings; see Tool 2 in this chapter),

what am I usually telling myself?

If I were in a cartoon, what would the bubble above my head be saying?

If there were a tape recorder in my head recording my every thought, what would it be saying when someone pushed "play?"

Example

I felt ...	...because I thought...
Annoyed	He should turn off his cell phone during the flight like everyone else.
Irritated	She shouldn't have lied to me. They went out to the movie and didn't invite me.
Furious	She shouldn't yell at her child.

Thoughts/Feelings Awareness Log

I felt ...	...because I thought...

"Autopilot" unhealthy coping skills frequently used to cope with anger often fit into one of two categories. Many people choose to internalize or "stuff" their anger, turning it inward and not expressing it. Others lash out in some way, expressing their anger externally. "Stuffers" may demonstrate other unhealthy coping skills down the road to deal with all the pent-up emotions. Examples of acting out often include yelling, destruction of property, or verbal or physical abuse. Spend a few minutes trying to identify unhealthy behavior habits you may have developed in response to these feelings.

The last time I felt angry I _____

When someone "gets under my skin," I usually _____

Others have told me my anger is a problem when I _____

Other things I have done in the past in an attempt to cope with feelings of anger that have in some way hurt me are

_____

_____

_____

_____

_____

Some of my "go-to"/"autopilot" "go-to"/"autopilot" anger coping skills are:

1.

2.

3.

4.

5.

Anger is perhaps the emotion that, when acted upon, creates the most significant long-term consequences. As has previously been touched upon, things that work in the short-term don't always work in the long term. In an attempt to increase your awareness, consider some of the ways in which your acting on anger has hurt you in the past. Enlisting the help of a support team member is often helpful is completing this exercise.

Example

Autopilot Coping Skill (from Tool 4)	Current or Past Negative Consequences
Yelled at girlfriend	Got dumped again
Snapped at boss	Got written up
Kicked hole in wall	Had to pay for repair, didn't have $ to go out that Friday

Awareness of Consequences Log

Autopilot Coping Skill (from Tool 4)	Current or Past Negative Consequences

Generally speaking, if you are a "stuffer," your problem with anger is more related to not being able to express feelings of anger at all. For people in this category, healthy coping involves getting feelings out in some form or fashion. Journaling, letter writing, and venting to a friend are often good places to start. If you are more prone to act out, your problem is not that you are not expressing your anger; it's that you are expressing it in a way that is counterproductive or hurting you in some way. For people in this category, the goal involves finding appropriate ways of expressing anger with less-damaging consequences. Skills in this category include yelling into a pillow, hitting a punching bag, writing an assertive letter, or doing something physical. Refer to your Tool 15 in Chapter 3 to get ideas, as anything involving physical exercise is especially helpful with anger.

Some things I will try the next time I feel anger are:

1.

2.

3.

4.

5.

6.

7.

8.

9.

10.

To reiterate, challenging distorted thoughts doesn't always make them go away, but it can put up enough of a "fight" that feelings aren't quite so intense that it may be at least slightly easier to use some of the skills you identified in Tool 6. Utilize the following *thought log* to attempt to *challenge* or generate some more *rational responses* to the distorted thoughts you identified in Tool 3. Remember, anger is the product of "shoulding" others, which, in essence, is the refusal to accept some aspect of reality. Therefore, the first challenge to every "should" is often a very simple reality-based statement of acceptance. Remember, accepting something is not the same as *condoning* it. It is simply acknowledging that "it is what it is."

Example

Distorted Thought	Rational Response
He should turn off his cell phone during the flight like everyone else.	I wish he would, but I can't make him. The plane isn't going to crash because of it. I can be thankful I have an aisle seat.
She shouldn't have lied to me. They really did go to that movie without me!	She did. She lied to me last month, too. I heard her lie to her mother yesterday. It's not reasonable for me to expect her to be honest. I know not to become too close a friend with her because I can't trust her. I can see the movie later with people I trust.
She shouldn't yell at her child.	She is yelling. There are a lot of parents who yell at their children. Just because she snapped doesn't mean she's abusive. If I believe she is, I can turn her in, and there are people who are paid to protect children. I have little say over how that child is raised but much influence on how my daughter gets raised. Maybe I'll go home and give her a hug.

Thought Log

Distorted Thought	Rational Response

As a refresher, *core beliefs* are deeply engrained beliefs that serve as filters through which we process information. All of our distorted thinking is the product of one or more harmful beliefs. This technique asks us to take a thought and continue to ask, "What would that mean about us if it were true?" until we get at the core belief is at the bottom of the distorted thought. If necessary, consult earlier in the chapter to note beliefs that often contribute to anger. Also, remember that many people need a therapist's help to assist with this for a period of time.

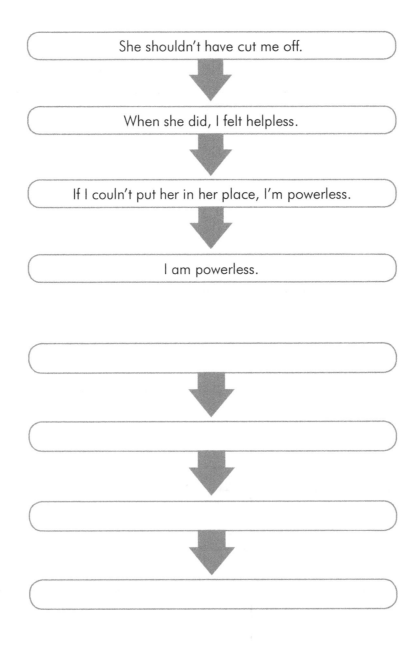

Remember, beliefs come in pairs. For each unhealthy belief you identified, formulate in your words what the exact opposite of that would mean to you. Flexible language remains important.

Example

My Beliefs

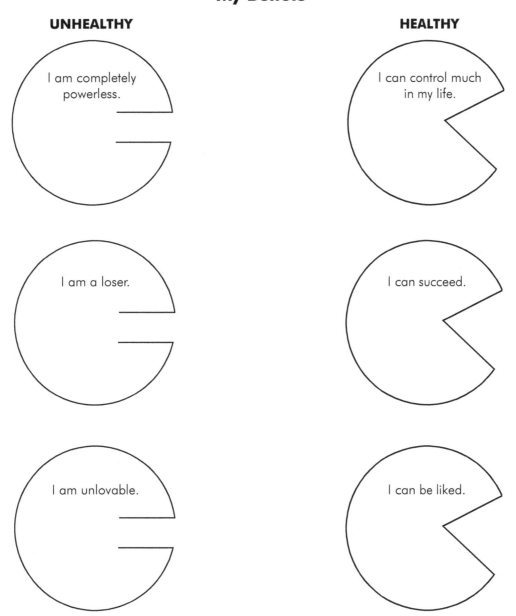

UNHEALTHY

I am completely powerless.

I am a loser.

I am unlovable.

HEALTHY

I can control much in my life.

I can succeed.

I can be liked.

My Beliefs

UNHEALTHY   HEALTHY

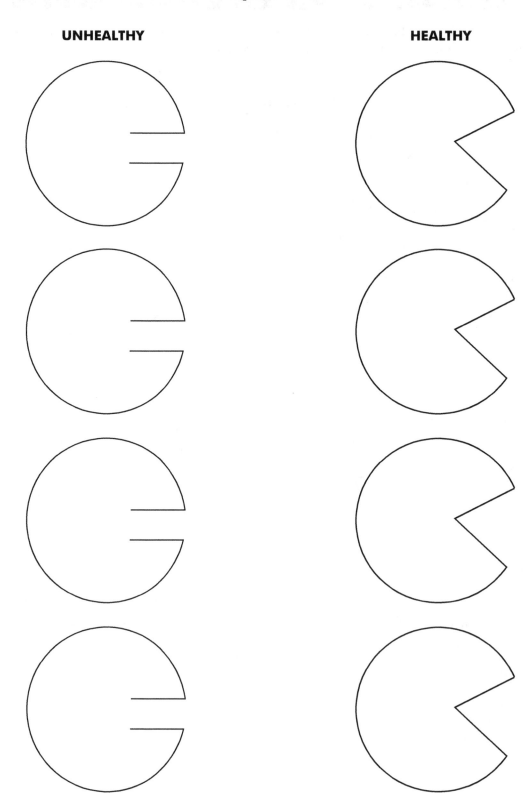

The strength of our beliefs significantly influences how often we feel stressful emotions and how strongly we experience them. Take a few minutes and try to assign a strength to each healthy and unhealthy belief. Usually, the easiest way is to use percentages so the total for unhealthy and healthy beliefs equals 100 percent.

Example

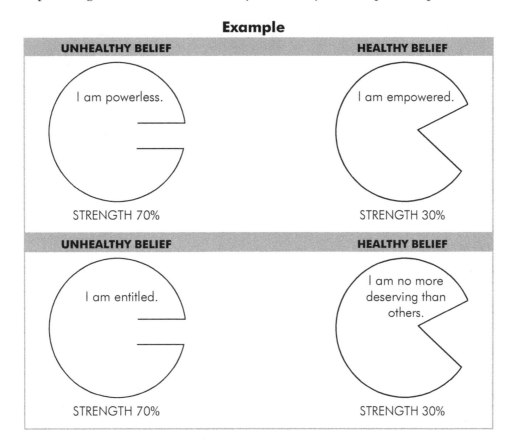

UNHEALTHY BELIEF	HEALTHY BELIEF
I am powerless.	I am empowered.
STRENGTH 70%	STRENGTH 30%
I am entitled.	I am no more deserving than others.
STRENGTH 70%	STRENGTH 30%

Rating the Strength of My Beliefs

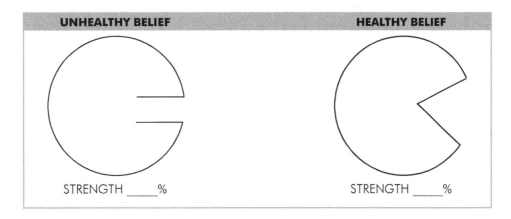

| UNHEALTHY BELIEF | HEALTHY BELIEF |
| STRENGTH _____% | STRENGTH _____% |

The following questions may be helpful in reflecting back on different periods of life to uncover some of the experiences you counted as evidence to support your belief (legs to hold up your table). You may need assistance from your therapist to get the most out of this tool.

The first time I ever remember feeling _____**[belief]**

was _____

The people in my life who influenced me to feel that way were:

Family members _____

_____

Friends/Peers _____

_____

Other significant people _____

_____

Experiences during my elementary school years _____

_____

_____

Experiences during my junior high years _____

_____

_____

Experiences during my high school years _____

_____

_____

Experiences during my college/young adult years _____

_____

_____

Significant experiences since then _____

_____

_____

Use the exercise to the left to try to insert some of the "evidence" from your past that you have "counted" to support each belief:

Example

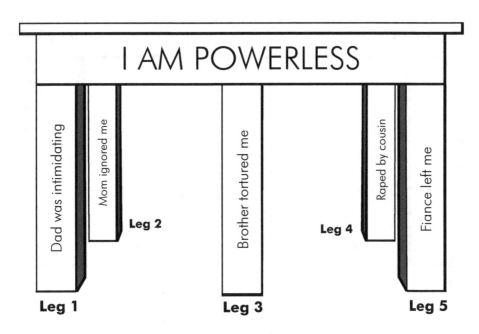

Evidence that I am powerless:

Leg 1: Dad intimidated everyone in the family, and I never had a say.

Leg 2: Mom ignored any request I had as child.

Leg 3: When I was young, my brothers would hold me down and torture me.

Leg 4: Raped at age 16 by older cousin.

Leg 5: Fiancé left me 3 weeks before our wedding after 2 years of dating and gave me no reason.

Unhealthy Evidence Log

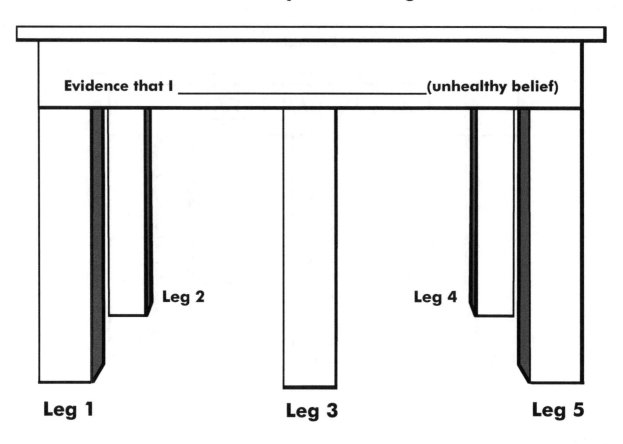

Evidence that I _____ **(unhealthy belief)**

Leg 2

Leg 4

Leg 1

Leg 3

Leg 5

Leg 1:

Leg 2:

Leg 3:

Leg 4:

Leg 5:

Because of how our filters are set up, we often notice instances that support our unhealthy beliefs more than we notice experiences that may support our opposite, healthy beliefs, but almost always, that "evidence" exists as well. Another valuable tool involves forcing ourselves to look back over those very same periods of life purposefully looking to see the evidence that supports our healthy beliefs. Many people rely on family members or friends who were around them during each period of life to help them "notice" such evidence. Again, even if they share things they see as "counting" that you don't think "should count" write them down anyway—you'll then have material to "add a but" to!

Example

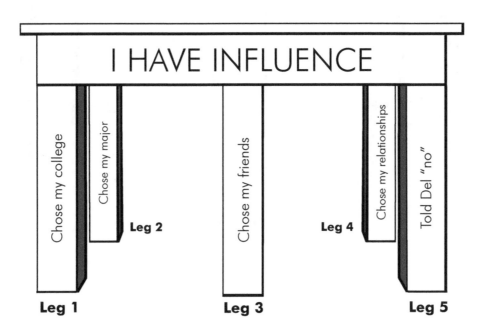

Evidence that I have some influences in my life:

Leg 1: I chose what college I went to.

Leg 2: I chose my major.

Leg 3: I chose my friends.

Leg 4: I chose whom I dated and married.

Leg 5: I told Del "no," and he is no longer in my life.

Healthy Evidence Log

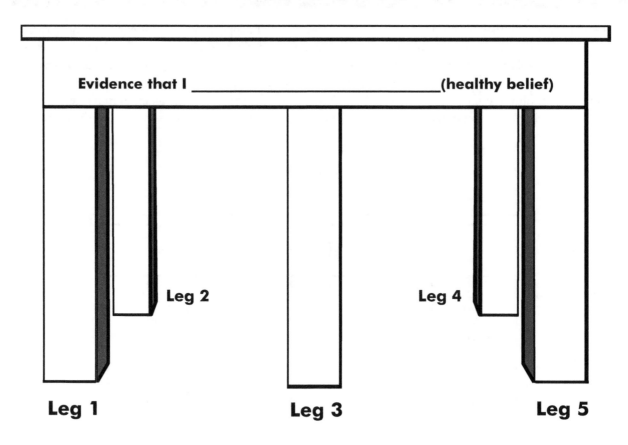

Evidence that I _____(healthy belief)

Leg 2

Leg 4

Leg 1

Leg 3

Leg 5

Leg 1:

Leg 2:

Leg 3:

Leg 4:

Leg 5:

TOOL 13 IDENTIFICATION OF COMPONENTS OF BELIEFS

Beliefs *mean* different things to different people. Refer to Tool 13 in Chapter 2 for examples of what it might mean to *have value*. Using that as a guide, compile a list of a few things that support your healthy beliefs about yourself.

Example

Belief

1. Can be empowered

Components

1. In charge of own body

2. Can control own choices

3. Can influence life circumstances

Belief

1.

Components

1.

2.

3.

2.

1.

2.

3.

3.

1.

2.

3.

Purposefully pay attention to things in life that might count as evidence that your healthy belief could be true.

Example

Evidence that I can be empowered

Date	Evidence
6/13	Chose to work out today
6/14	Told friend preference of movie
6/16	Chose where we ate lunch
6/18	Decided to stay home and not go to the party Jeremy was pressuring me to go to
6/21	Wrote letter protesting animal abuse

I AM
EMPOWERED

Evidence that I can be _____ (healthy belief) log

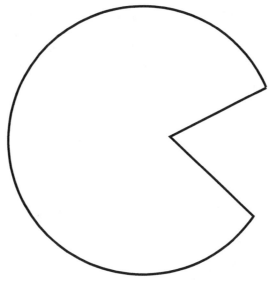

Date	Evidence

Self-monitoring is an important tool to use in managing anger. Some people go from "0 to 60 in 2 seconds," and others feel anger building gradually. Many people aren't aware of when their anger intensifies, or of behaviors they turn to as a result of feeling angry. The tool of self-monitoring will help you learn to observe your own feelings and behavior more accurately. Observing and recording feelings and behavior helps immediately, as you can become more aware of when anger is present and its impact on your actions. Self-monitoring does not come easily, and most people believe they are better at it than they really are.

Self-monitoring takes practice. Perhaps the easiest way to get started is to start with behaviors you have no desire to change. Some people start with going to the bathroom, brushing their teeth, or getting in their car. Start by observing *frequency* and *duration*; that is, how *often* you do the behavior, and once you do it, how *long* the behavior continues. Some people are painfully aware of behaviors that need modifying, while others have less insight. Also, because anger is experienced on a continuum, some people may often not "count" anger as anger because "it wasn't that bad." Just as when someone trying to lose weight may say, "That bite of cake didn't count because it was just one bite," people dealing with anger may often deny "smaller" manifestations of anger. In doing so, they lose objectivity with regard to observing their anger. One helpful strategy involves enlisting a person whom you trust and frequently spend time with to assist you. Ask him or her to monitor your behavior independent of your monitoring efforts, and at the end of the week, compare the friend's log with yours. If there is a large discrepancy between his or her log and yours, this is a sign you may not be observing your behaviors accurately.

A final tip is to find a way of recording behaviors as they occur. Many people carry a golf counter or use their smartphone or other electronic device that they always carry, so as not to forget to record incidents. Once you get better at observing your behavior, then you can begin observing your anger itself.

Examples
Angry Behavior Monitoring

Date	Behavior	Frequency	Duration
7/2	Temper tantrum	2x	5 min, 2 min

Angry Feelings Monitoring

Date	Event/Trigger	Intensity	Duration
12/3	Boss yelled at me	8	20 min

Angry Behavior Monitoring

Date	Behavior	Frequency	Duration

Angry Feelings Monitoring

Date	Event/Trigger	Intensity	Duration

Anger has everything to do with our values. You may remember that anger is always a product of "should statements" toward others. When do we "should?" When someone else violates our values. Actually, whenever we violate our own values, we "should" ourselves and feel guilty. When others violate our values, we "should" them and feel angry. For that reason, it is vital to know what our values are. You may be able to make some connections between your values and your triggers. People value things differently; thus, some triggers that might infuriate one person don't affect others in the slightest. Take a few minutes and list your values. Note that values often change throughout a person's life.

Example

My Values

1. Kindness

2. Honesty

3. Education

4. The environment

5. Respect for authority

My Values

1.

2.

3.

4.

5.

Once you have identified your values, you can try to connect your episodes of anger with specific values that have been violated and the "should statement" that resulted from it.

Values Log

Date	Event	Value Violated	Should Statement
7/3	Kid next to me ignored the flight attendant's instruction to turn off electronic devices	Respect for Authority	"He should turn off his cell phone during the flight like everyone else."
7/10	Friend Joni told me she did not want to go to a movie—then went with my friends without inviting me	Honesty	"She shouldn't have lied to me. They really did go to that movie without me!"
7/13	Saw woman in restaurant yelling at child	Kindness	"She shouldn't yell at her child."

Date	Event	Value Violated	Should Statement

The next step is to realize that we have *zero* control over other people's behavior but 100 percent control over our own behavior. Therefore, all we can do is live our lives in ways that do support our values. We can then be purposeful about making decisions consistent with those values. Use the following log to monitor your behaviors through the lens of your values.

Values Monitor

Date	Value	Behavior
4/21	Kindness	Went out of my way to thank my mother
4/24	Honesty	Said no when friend offered me test answers so I could cheat with her

Date	Value	Behavior

There is nothing new or original about this tool. In fact, people have probably been using the time-out technique for centuries. It is most commonly associated with modifying children's behavior, but it may be one of the most important strategies for managing anger for adults as well. Failure to be able to use this technique in moments when it would be useful has resulted in hurt feelings, wounded relationships, destruction of property, and prison sentences. Many people can recognize how this may be helpful in times when they are not "in the moment" but are incapable of using it in times when they really need to. Using this tool requires some degree of mastery of previous tools, including self-monitoring. If we do not realize how angry we are getting or what behaviors our dysfunctional thoughts are tempting us to do, we often don't realize until it's too late that it's time to take a time-out. For this reason, awareness of one's anger style is important. For instance, if you are a person whose anger builds slowly over time, you probably can afford to postpone taking a time-out longer than others. Conversely, if you are an impulsive person who can go "from 0 to 60" in a matter of seconds, it is probably more important for you to take a time-out, even as early as when you recognize that your anger is a "1" or a "2."

Tips for Taking a Time-Out

Do remove yourself from the upsetting situation before you act in a way that could create unwanted consequences.

Do stay gone long enough to cool down . In some cases, this may mean an hour. Other circumstances may require staying away for a day or more.

Don't use alcohol or drugs while in your "time-out."

Do use distraction initially. Force yourself to think about something else to help decrease your level of physical arousal so that you can think more clearly. It is important *not* to tell yourself "Don't think about this," or it is likely you will continue to. Rather, identify other things *to* think about to consume your thoughts. Examples could include planning a vacation, surfing the Internet, counting to 100, or immersing yourself in a movie, football game, or other visual activity that requires your attention.

If you aren't able to concentrate, **do** something physical: Go for a walk, run, bike ride, garden—anything physical can be helpful.

Once you calm down, **do** try to think rationally how to resolve the situation.

If necessary, **do** consult a friend or person you trust.

Do get validated. Find someone who can validate your feelings and understand where you are coming from and constructively encourage you how to respond.

Don't find "yes men" (or "yes women") who will "fuel your shoulds." These people seem validating initially but only serve to "add fuel to the fire" and make us more angry at the person we are already angry at— which is not helpful in the long run if we want or need to maintain an ongoing relationship with that person.

Don't use the time-out as an excuse to avoid completely situations that need to be dealt with. The purpose of the time-out is to *temporarily* remove yourself so you *can* go back and deal with the situation, *not* to *permanently* avoid it, Many people try to avoid dealing with such situations, but this keeps conflict unresolved and allows anger to continue to simmer.

One tool that is useful for helping to vent feelings involves writing an assertive letter. This tool can take several different forms and can be utilized in different ways. One helpful way of approaching this is to write two letters with different purposes. The first is simply to *vent angry feelings*. This is never intended for the person you are angry at to see. In this letter, be as honest as you can be. Use whatever language you need to use. These letters often aren't pretty! Then, review the letter with a therapist or friend. Decide if there is value in the other person receiving a version of the letter. If you decide there is, modify the letter with a new intent: saying what you believe you need to say in a way that you think the person can hear it. Such a letter then needs to be followed up with a phone call, email, or person-to-person conversation. Consult with your therapist regarding which is the best way to proceed in your particular situation. Following is a format that many have found helpful for this type of letter. This is just a guideline. You may omit emotions that do not apply or add emotions or descriptions that are not included. This is just to get you started. Use language with which you are comfortable.

Letter Format

Dear _____**,**

Feeling	Assertive Expression
Anger	"I don't like it when …" "I hate it when …" "It frustrates me when …" "It infuriates me when you …."
Depression	"I feel sad when …" "It hurts when …" "I feel lonely because …"
Anxiety	"It scares me when you …" "I am afraid of …" "I worry the most about …"
Guilt	"I'm sorry that …" "I feel like I should have …" "I do regret …"
Love	"I love you because …" "I appreciate that you …" "I understand that …" "I respect you because …" "I need you in my life for …"

Sincerely, _____

P.S. What I need from you is _____

_____

Many people hear the term *forgiveness* and are immediately turned off. There are probably a number of reasons for this, but I would submit that if that is your reaction to it, it is probably a sign that doing some forgiveness work could be beneficial for you. I have often heard people say things like. "Forgiveness—that's spiritual stuff!" While forgiveness can have spiritual components, it is a vital tool to effectively deal with anger. *Resentment* (emotional word) and *unforgiveness* (spiritual word) mean essentially the same thing: *anger held onto.* Anger, at any level, that we choose to hold onto fits into this category and contributes to staying unhealthy. Thousands of books have been written on the topic of forgiveness. Comprehensively covering this topic is far outside the scope of this tool. However, examining the role of unforgiveness in unresolved anger can be a powerful tool in recovery. The Bible teaches forgiveness. Most major world religions place an emphasis on forgiveness. Why? Probably because it's good for us! If it is obviously good for us, why do so many people resist it? There are many distorted thoughts associated with an unwillingness to initiate the practice of forgiveness. Identifying and rationally responding to some of these is the goal of this tool.

Example

Forgiveness Thought Log

Distorted Unforgiveness Thought	Rational Response
I will not give him the satisfaction of my forgiveness.	Forgiveness is not for them—it is for me. The old adage says, "Unforgiveness is like swallowing a drop of poison every day waiting for the other person to die." I will not continue to give him control over my life now that I have a choice.
Forgiveness is like saying what she did to me is OK.	Forgiveness is not saying that at all. Forgiveness is saying what they did is still as unacceptable as it was the day they did it to me but that I am choosing not to hold it against them any longer—for my sake.
Forgive and forget—and since I don't think I can forget, then I must not be able to forgive.	There are some things in life I will never forget. Actually, if I forget, I may not learn from past situations. Just because I will never forget has nothing to do with my ability to forgive.
If I forgive him that means I have to trust him again, and there's no way that's happening.	Forgiveness is about the past. Trust is about the future. I can forgive him but never trust him again. Forgiveness is always healthy for me, regardless of his behavior, but trust is earned. I can forgive and still set whatever boundaries I want with him.
I'm just not ready to forgive yet—I'll forgive when I feel like it.	Anger comes from shoulds. Forgiving means working to give up my shoulds. So, until I start working on it, I'll never get around to feeling like it. Forgiveness is first granted, then felt.

Forgiveness Thought Log

Distorted Unforgiveness Thought	Rational Response
I'll forgive her when she apologizes to me.	It may be easier if she apologizes, but what if she never does? If I tell myself I will not take steps to better myself until she does—and perhaps she never will—then I'm continuing to give her the power to keep me miserable. I will no longer give her that.
Time heals all wounds. I don't have to do anything—it will just get better with time.	Time can help me think about a situation more objectively, but the reality is I can hold a grudge as long as I want to. If time is all it took, no one would go to their grave angry. If I don't want to be one of those people, I have to actually initiate and participate in the forgiveness process. It takes work, but it will be worth it.

Identify and rationally respond to your own distorted thoughts preventing you from beginning your process of forgiveness.

Forgiveness Thought Log

Distorted Unforgiveness Thought	Rational Response

Once you have dealt with your thoughts that may have kept you from beginning the process of forgiveness, you are ready to start. People practice forgiveness in many ways. Some steps you may want to consider to get you started but are not limited to are as follows.

Example

Forgiveness Steps

1. Journal
2. Pray
3. Meditate
4. Talk to my therapist
5. Talk to my priest
6. Challenge my "shoulds" daily
7. Practice acceptance
8. Try to empathize
9. Go to church
10. Get reinvolved with my support group and sponsor

My Forgiveness Steps

1.

2.

3.

4.

5.

6.

7.

8.

9.

10.

Now, to help you with those "heat of the moment" reactions, refer to Tool 20 in Chapter 2 to develop your cards. Remember, the coping card gives you alternative things to *do* "in the moment." Cue cards help you with how to *think*.

Example

When I feel _____*enraged*_____ (behavior from Tool 4),

I can (choices from Tool 6):

1. *Go for a run*

2. *Take a time-out*

3. *Write an assertive letter and vent to my therapist*

Your Coping Card

When I feel _____ (behavior from Tool 4),

I can (choices from Tool 6):

1. _____

2. _____

3. _____

Example

Cognitive Cue Card

Just because <u>he yelled at me</u> **doesn't mean** <u>I'm completely powerless.</u>

<u>I have a lot of control over important areas in my life.</u>

I know <u>I can feel empowered</u> **is true because** <u>there are a lot of other</u>

<u>more important areas of my life that I can control.</u>

Your Cognitive Cue Card

Cognitive Cue Card

Just because _____**doesn't mean** _____

_____

I know _____ **is true because**_____

_____

Chapter 11 **Other Impulsive/Destructive Behaviors**

COMMON BELIEFS

- Insufficient self-control

COMMON DISTORTIONS

- Rationalization

COMMON AUTOMATIC THOUGHTS

- "I have to have it now."
- "I can't wait."
- "I have no self-control."
- "I can't delay gratification."

COMMON FEELINGS

- Increased sense of urgency
- Physiological adrenaline rush
- Decreased conviction

COMMON BEHAVIORS

- Impulsive (unplanned) substance use
- Sexual promiscuity
- Binge or other "emotional eating"
- Reckless driving, spending/shopping sprees
- Other self-harming behaviors

INSUFFICIENT SELF-CONTROL

People do "impulsive" and "destructive" behaviors for different reasons. A tool later in this chapter is provided to help you examine your specific motivations for engaging in these behaviors. Many people who were born with highly sensitive temperaments and experience emotions more intensely than others do are prone to feeling the need to do something to get a quick "feel-good" response. These behaviors frequently follow relational triggers (e.g, hurtful comments, rejections, feelings of intense anger). Take a few minutes to answer the following questions that may give you a window into your impulsive or destructive behaviors.

The last time I acted impulsively or destructively was _____

I did it in response to _____

The emotion I was feeling prior to engaging in this behavior was _____

Themes in times I act impulsively are _____

Things that seem to happen right before I act this way are _____

My impulsive/destructive behavior triggers are:

1.

2.

3.

4.

5.

Some people are very good at expressing their feelings. Others have difficulty recognizing or giving names to feelings or even recognizing that they have emotions at all. The "Feelings Face Sheet" included in Tool 2 in Chapter 2 is often helpful for aiding people in identifying what feelings they are actually having. Using the face sheet as your guide, pick out several emotions that seem to describe best what you experience immediately prior to engaging in impulsive or destructive behaviors.

Feelings Log

Type of Feeling	Mon	Tues	Wed	Thurs	Fri	Sat	Sun
Happy							
Sad							
Excited							
Angry							
Irritated							
Frustrated							
Proud							
Regretful							
Disgusted							
Excited							
Guilty							
Ashamed							
Anxious							
Confident							
Resentful							
Gloomy							
Fearful							
Scared							
Panicked							
Grateful							
Loved							
Envious							
Jealous							
Compassionate							
Affectionate							

Feelings that precipitate my impulsive/destructive behaviors are:

1.   **3.**   **5.**

2.   **4.**

Some therapists may use the term *irrational thoughts*. Others prefer the term *dysfunctional thought*s or *maladaptive thoughts*. The advantage of thinking of thoughts as dysfunctional is recognizing that thoughts that were functional or helpful in one setting may become dysfunctional or hurtful in other settings. For instance, someone who grew up in an abusive family might have learned through experience that, "If I speak up, somebody gets hit or yelled at, or someone leaves, so it's best that I just never speak up." Now, if someone really did get hurt every time he opened his mouth, it would be adaptive to keep his mouth shut. But, if that person adopts that way of thinking ("It's best that I just keep my mouth shut") even after he has grown up and left that home, it is not functional or adaptive and will not lead to effective outcomes. Thus, what is functional in one setting is not necessarily helpful in other contexts. Other professionals may use the term *distorted thinking*. This is the term this workbook uses. Distorted thoughts might be defined as any thoughts that in get in the way of our feeling and behaving in healthy manners.

When _____(trigger; see **Tool 1 in this chapter**) **happens,**

and I feel _____(feelings; see **Tool 2 in this chapter**),

what am I usually telling myself?

If I were in a cartoon, what would the bubble above my head be saying?

If there were a tape recorder in my head recording my every thought, what would it be saying when someone pushed "play?"

Example

I felt ...	...because I thought...
Vengeful	It's OK to act spiteful because she made me mad.
Sense of urgency	I have to have that item now.
Unmotivated	It's OK to binge, because I felt upset—food will soothe me, and nothing else will help. I can't stand feeling this way.

Thoughts/Feelings Awareness Log

I felt ...	...because I thought...

TOOL 4 GENERATE LIST OF UNHEALTHY "GO-TO" COPING SKILLS

Most people develop a set of standard "go-to" coping skills when they feel that need for a quick "feel good." Perhaps you have heard the term *autopilot*, referring to just falling back on the same old skills that in some way feel comfortable but often don't help. Usually, these behaviors "worked" in the past but no longer work in the present. Also, some may continue to work in the short term but be making problems worse in the long term. A few such examples people turn to include alcohol, drugs, promiscuous sex, spending, or shopping to get that "quick fix." Before figuring out healthy skills to use when these urges creep up, it is often useful to generate a list of what we have been trying that has *not* been working.

The last time I acted impulsively, I _____

Other things I have done in the past in an attempt to cope that have in some way hurt me

are _____

_____

_____

_____

_____

Some of my "go-to"/"autopilot" coping skills are:

1.

2.

3.

4.

5.

As Tool 4 touched on, things that worked in the past don't always work in the present, and things that work in the present in the short term don't always work in the long term. Some people have little to no awareness as to how their past coping choices have impacted their present life circumstances. Others fully recognize that their present choices may cause future consequences but continue to choose that "quick feel-good" behavior regardless. One tool that often helps motivate people to change is taking a close look at how their past behaviors have contributed to present undesirable situations. When considering consequences for autopilot behaviors, keep in mind consequences can take many forms.

Example

Autopilot Coping Skill (from Tool 4)	Current or Past Negative Consequences
Told best friend's boyfriend she cheated on him	She's mad at me, he told his friends to stay away from me, and I am alone
Ate six bags of chips in 1 hour	Gained 10 lb past week, lower self-esteem, increased depression

Awareness of Consequences Log

Autopilot Coping Skill (from Tool 4)	Current or Past Negative Consequences

Maybe you've heard it said that "Change = Insight + Action." While it is true that many people never develop insight into their unhealthy behaviors, it's also true that many people do develop insight into unhealthy behaviors but never take action to change them! Perhaps you have also heard Albert Einstein's definition of insanity: *doing the same thing over and over again expecting a different result!* For instance, some people recognize that their romantic partner "picker" is broken, but continue to select unhealthy men or women to be with. Millions of people now recognize that smoking has many health hazards but refuse to quit. The reality is that if we want things to get better in our lives, we have to be willing to try something different! Fortune telling gets in the way and convinces us "this won't work because … ." However, the reality is, until we try, we won't know. We may try a new skill and find it doesn't work either, but at least we tried. We can now add it to the list of skills we already know don't work and move on to try something else. It is kind of like trying on new shoes: If one pair doesn't fit, no harm done. We can just put them in the pile that won't work for us and keep trying. Refer to your list of coping skills and pick some things you are willing to try next time you feel an urge to engage in an impulsive or destructive behavior.

Some things I will try the next time I feel an urge to act impulsively are:

1.

2.

3.

4.

5.

In the same way that recognizing but continuing to engage in unhealthy behaviors rarely gets us far along in recovery, recognizing distorted thoughts but not changing them also keeps us stuck. Recognizing and identifying these thoughts is an important first step, but if we don't rigorously challenge them, we will continue to suffer those same horrible feelings we have about ourselves, which will make it more difficult to not revert to those autopilot behaviors. Challenging distorted thoughts doesn't always make them go away but can put up enough of a "fight" that feelings aren't quite so intense that it may be at least slightly easier to use some of the skills you identified in Tool 6. Utilize the following *thought log* to attempt to *challenge* or generate some more *rational responses* to the distorted thoughts you identified in Tool 3.

Example

Distorted Thought	Rational Response
It's OK to act spiteful because she upset me.	It's not OK. I am working toward building healthy relationships. I am angry, but acting this way would only hurt me and sabotage my goals.
I have to have that item now.	I want it, but I don't need it. We need $ for prescriptions. We can't afford it. I can walk away.
It's OK to binge eat because I felt upset. Food will soothe, me and nothing else will help. I can't stand to feel this way.	It's not OK to binge for any reason. I can now tolerate intense emotions better than before. I'll hate myself afterward. I'll feel fat. I'll feel depressed. I have other skills I can use.

Thought Log

Distorted Thought	Rational Response

As mentioned in Chapter 1, *core beliefs* are deeply ingrained beliefs that we have in different areas of life (self, others, and the world). They serve as "filters" through which we process information. Because we all have had different life experiences, our filters are unique. It is because of these filters that we may perceive things differently. Thus, two people can go through the same event and come out of it with a different experience. Filters contribute to different thoughts, feelings, and responses. One tool that can help identify core beliefs is the *downward arrow* technique. This technique asks us to take a thought and continue to ask, "What would that mean about us if it were true?" until we get at the core belief at the bottom of the distorted thought. Note the following example, and then try one on your own. Many people need a therapist's help to assist with this for a period of time.

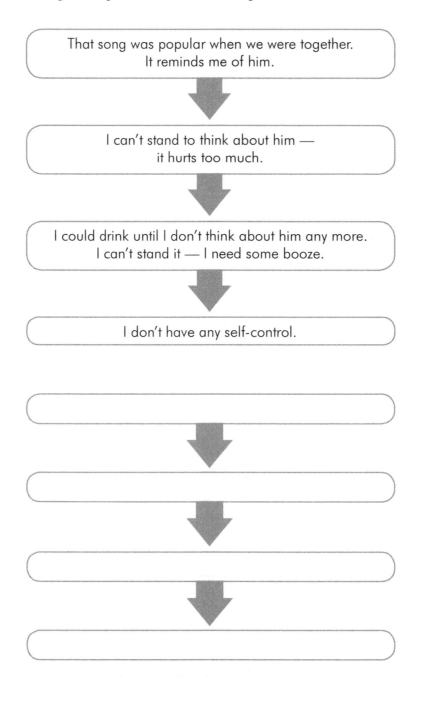

It's similar to when we take our car into the shop: The mechanic never tells us about the 300 and some things that *are working*. He tells us about the one or two that are not, because that is why we had to bring the car in to begin with. Similarly, in therapy, the focus is often on the unhealthy beliefs, but *the reality is that beliefs come in pairs*. For every unhealthy belief, we all have an opposite, healthy belief. For instance, if you identified the insufficient self-control belief (always present in impulse control–related behaviors) you may want to identify your opposite healthy belief as something like, *"I can wait"* or *"I can have self control."* Take a few minutes and decide how you want to word your healthy alternate belief.

Example

My Beliefs

UNHEALTHY   **HEALTHY**

I have to have it now.   I can show self-control.

Just because we believe something doesn't mean we believe it 100 percent. For instance, there are people who are convinced (100 percent belief) that there is life on other planets. There are people who are certain there is not (0 percent belief). Others may believe it is *possible* but not likely (maybe 10 percent belief). Similarly, some people believe they can control their impulses all the time, some of the time, or never. The strength of our beliefs significantly influences how often we feel certain emotions and how strongly we experience them. Take a few minutes and try to assign a strength to each healthy and unhealthy belief. Usually, the easiest way is to use percentages so the total for unhealthy and healthy beliefs equals 100 percent.

Example

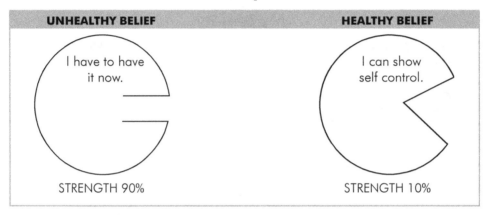

Rating the Strength of My Beliefs

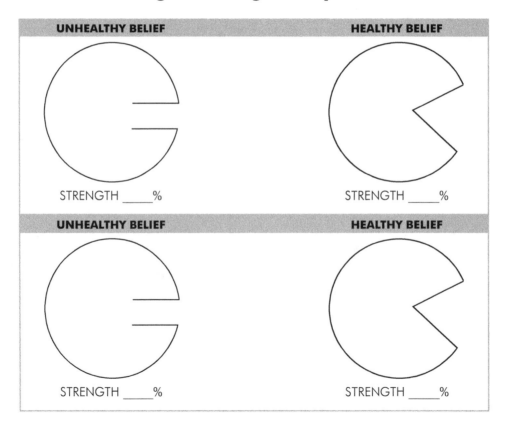

Leslie Sokol, a faculty member at the Beck Institute, compares a belief to a tabletop: In the same way that tabletops need legs to hold them up, beliefs need legs or "evidence" to support them. *"Evidence"* is in quotation marks, because different people *count* evidence differently. For instance, some people who believe in aliens may have heard the same stories (information) as people who do not, but for various reasons, one person "counts" it as "evidence," and the other does not. The same holds true for beliefs about ourselves. Anyone who has a failure belief about themselves, whether they realize it or not, has collected "evidence" that they have "counted" over the years to support that belief. This exercise can be a little more time consuming and emotionally draining than some of the previous ones but can be a powerful tool for recovery.

The following questions may be helpful in reflecting back on different periods of your life to uncover some of the experiences you counted as evidence to support your belief (legs to hold up your table). You may need assistance from your therapist to get the most out of this tool.

The first time I ever remember feeling _____[belief]

was _____

The people in my life who influenced me to feel that way were:

Family members _____

_____

Friends/Peers _____

_____

Other significant people _____

_____

Experiences during my elementary school years _____

_____

Experiences during my junior high years _____

_____

Experiences during my high school years _____

_____

_____

Experiences during my college/young adult years _____

_____

_____

Significant experiences since then _____

_____

_____

Use the exercise on the previous page to try to insert some of the "evidence" from your past that you have "counted" to support each belief:

Example

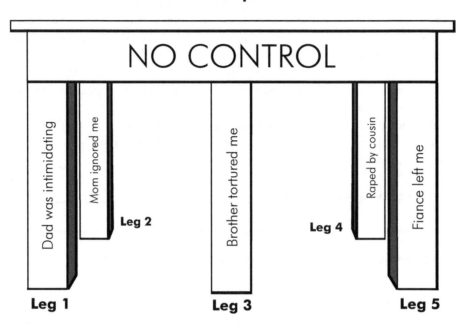

NO CONTROL

Dad was intimidating — Leg 1

Mom ignored me — Leg 2

Brother tortured me — Leg 3

Raped by cousin — Leg 4

Fiance left me — Leg 5

Evidence that I couln't control my inpulses:

Leg 1: I couldn't stand pain of divorce

Leg 2: Felt I had to drink.

Leg 3: Peer pressured to smoke pot.

Leg 4: Felt need to be loved.

Leg 5: Had sex at first opportunity.

Unhealthy Evidence Log

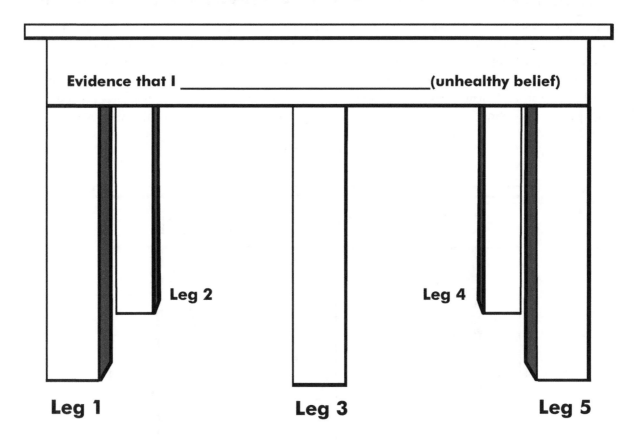

Evidence that I _____(unhealthy belief)

Leg 2

Leg 4

Leg 1

Leg 3

Leg 5

Leg 1:

Leg 2:

Leg 3:

Leg 4:

Leg 5:

Because of how these filters (our beliefs) are set up, we often notice instances that support the unhealthy beliefs more than we notice experiences that may support our opposite, healthy beliefs, but almost always, that "evidence" exists as well. One valuable tool involves forcing ourselves to look back over those very same periods of life, purposefully looking to see the evidence that supports our healthy beliefs. Many people rely on family members or friends who were around them during each period of life to help them "notice" such evidence. Even if they share things they see as "counting" that you don't think "should count," write them down anyway—you can *add a but* (Chapter 2, Tool 16) later.

Example

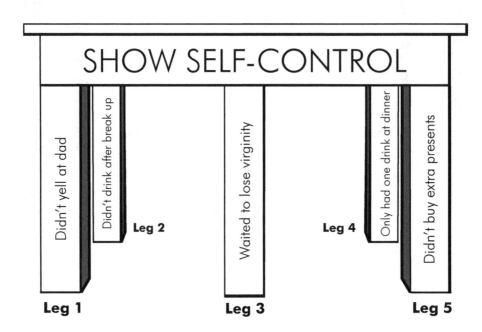

Evidence that I can show self-control:

Leg 1: Was tempted to yell at my dad when he grounded me in the 9th grade but didn't

Leg 2: Wanted to drink until I was numb when first boyfriend broke up with me but didn't

Leg 3: Had chance to lose my virginity at age 16 but decided not to and said no

Leg 4: Tempted to buy extra presents for Christmas but didn't

Leg 5: Only had one margarita with Mexican food

Healthy Evidence Log

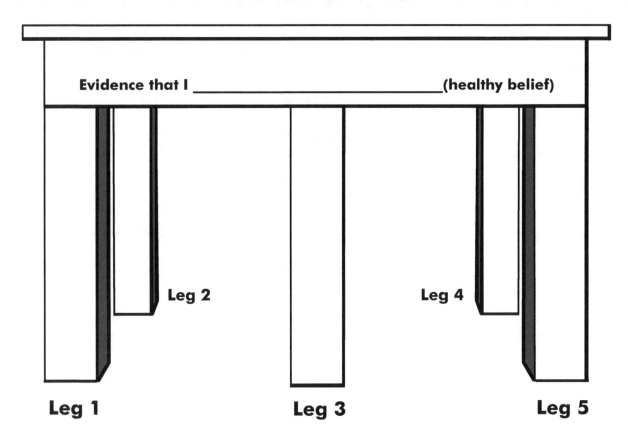

Evidence that I _____(healthy belief)

Leg 2

Leg 4

Leg 1

Leg 3

Leg 5

Leg 1:

Leg 2:

Leg 3:

Leg 4:

Leg 5:

Beliefs *mean* different things to different people. In terms of the insufficient self-control belief, some people have trouble controlling their behavior in only one area, such as with alcohol. Others struggle with two, three, or many behaviors. Identify the areas in which your lack of self-control manifests itself.

Example

Belief

1. Can show self-control

Components

1. Alcohol

2. Spending

3. Emotional eating

Belief

1.

Components

1.

2.

3.

2.

1.

2.

3.

3.

1.

2.

3.

Another important tool for developing more healthy beliefs and thus becoming less reactive is ongoing evidence logs. Whereas previous tools asked you to review your life and look for "evidence" from the past, *ongoing evidence logs* ask you to be mindful of evidence in your everyday life. Because your unhealthy filters will naturally be pointing you toward negative evidence, it is often necessary to purposefully seek out positive evidence. *Purposefully seek out* doesn't mean "make it up" if it legitimately isn't there but, rather, means to try to pay attention to any evidence that legitimately may be present but missed due to your unhealthy filter. This tool requires you to identify those areas in which you are tempted (Tool 13) and notice times you had a "temptation thought" but chose not to act on it.

Example

Evidence that I can demonstrate self-control:

Date	Evidence
12/12	Drank no alcohol at Christmas Party
12/13	Only had one margarita with Mexican food
12/16	Stayed within budget at mall
12/20	Tempted to buy extra presents but didn't
12/24	Chose not to eat pie at Christmas dinner

I CAN
DEMONSTRATE
SELF-CONTROL

Evidence that I can demonstrate self control:

Date	Evidence

Once you have identified what your triggers and unhealthy autopilot behaviors are, the next step is getting better "in the moment" at not acting on your urges. Cards (Tool 20) are helpful with this. When you recognize a "button" has been pushed and you sense some of the red flags for engaging in an impulsive or destructive behavior, the first step is to *safeguard your environment*. This simply means doing anything you can that will make it less likely for you to engage in the behavior. Some safeguarding can be done preemptively. For instance, if you are in your first month without alcohol trying to break a 20-year habit, you can ensure your safety by not keeping any alcohol in the house. Other safeguarding must be done "in the moment," which is much harder. For people who have urges to self-harm in some way, it means making sure all objects that could be used to do so are removed. For people who are having suicidal thoughts, it might mean having high-lethality medications locked up under someone else's supervision. If you are having an urge to binge eat and you have the food you like to binge on at the house (for some necessary reason), it may mean your leaving the house. If your urge is to spend, you could limit your access to funds. Depending on the area your unhealthy urge involves, your steps will be different. Spend some time considering specific areas for which you may need to safeguard and what that might look like for you.

Areas it would be helpful for me to consider safeguarding are

_____

_____

_____

Specific steps I could take preemptively (ahead of time) that would make my environment safer and less tempting are

_____

_____

_____

Things I could do "in the moment" to safeguard when an urge overcomes me are

_____

_____

_____

For me, safeguarding might include _____

_____

_____

_____

A coping skill can be defined as *any solution one uses in an attempt to solve a problem*. Coping skills may be "bad" (maladaptive, dysfunctional, destructive) or "good" (adaptive, functional, helpful). Review the "balanced person" sections in the stress management chapter (Chapter 3, tools 15–19) to remind yourself of healthy coping skills. A *distraction technique* can be defined as any coping skill that *requires* you to think. Examples might include counting to 10, calling a friend, reciting the alphabet, listening to music, and watching TV (if you are actually following the lyrics or plot—you can't just "veg"). These skills are based on the principle that you can only think one thought at a time. Your thoughts may be racing or going back and forth between two or more thoughts or swirling through your head like a tornado, but you can only think one thought at a time. Sometimes, people have thoughts that are racing or "swarming" to the point that they *feel* like they are not able to change them. When this is the case, rather than attempt to evaluate them, it can be helpful to simply distract yourself. While this doesn't help restructure or "retrain" your thoughts, it can give your mind a break from moments of intensity. Some people think of thoughts as the tape that is playing over and over in their heads. Distracting oneself can be similar to "changing the channel" in your mind to help lower the intensity of what you are feeling. This is not a skill we want to use on a regular basis or it simply becomes a way to avoid feelings altogether, but if you are tempted to do something destructive, distraction is often better than the alternative! Consider some coping skills that inherently require thought, and assemble a list of distraction techniques.

My Distraction Techniques

1.

2.

3.

4.

5.

When an infant is screaming, what most frequently calms him or her down? A warm bottle, a mother's arms, or a warm blanket? All are attempts to *soothe*. When we are children, it is our parents' job to meet our needs and come up with ways to soothe us. As adults, it is *our* job to figure out ways to soothe ourselves, and when emotions are at their highest, this is often a difficult chore. Because some people experience strong emotions more frequently than others, having a set of skills designed to soothe is extremely important. These tools might include taking a warm bath, getting a massage, drinking a cup of hot tea, listening to calming music, or burning incense, to name just a few. Many patients who struggle with intense emotions resort to impulsive or destructive behaviors to create a "release" of these feelings because they have not adequately learned to soothe themselves. Spend a few minutes considering behaviors from your coping skills list that might have a *soothing* or *calming* effect on you.

My Soothing Strategies

1.

2.

3.

4.

5.

Transitional objects are inanimate objects that people can become attached to and gain comfort from. These objects often remind them of a person of importance in the absence of that person. Children often have a "special toy" or blanket that is associated with a parent or grandparent. I had a patient who purchased a small figure that she kept in her pocket at all times that she called her "pocket Jeff." At times when she was considering an impulsive or destructive behavior, she would pull it out and remember what we were working on. Transitional objects may include gifts, stuffed animals, a rosary, or any other object with some meaning that can provide comfort in times of emotional turmoil.

Do I have currently use a transitional object? _____

_____

If not, is this something that may be helpful for me? _____

_____

A person of importance connected to this for me might be _____

_____

What might I consider using as a transitional object? _____

_____

For individuals who experience intense and seemingly unbearable emotions, an important part of coping effectively at times simply involves "weathering the storm." Some days, the goal is not self-growth but simply survival—and to survive without acting on those intense emotions in ways that hurt oneself in the long run. Dr. Marsha Linehan, the founder of Dialectical Behavior Therapy (DBT), wrote on the importance of patients' ability to just get by and created an acronym to describe several ways to "IMPROVE the moment." The following list was adapted from *Cognitive-Behavioral Treatment of Borderline Personality Disorder* by Marsha M. Linehan, 1993.

Imagery
- Find a "safe place"

Meaning
- Read Victor Frankl
- Be inspired by Florence Griffith Joyner
- Find reasons for living

Prayer
- Seek divine comfort
- Pray for strength
- Pray for meaning
- Turn things over to God

Relaxation
- Do deep breathing
- Listen to relaxing music
- Do progressive muscle relaxation (tapes can be purchased)

One thing in the moment
- Focus on one thing
- Practice mindfulness
- Perform grounding techniques

Vacation
- Take short trips/plan regular getaways as stress management
- Find relaxing places (e.g., comfy chair, nearby park)
- Encouragement
- Call member of support team
- Read Bible or meaningful religious verses or affirmations
- Engage in positive self-talk

Five ways I could IMPROVE the moment are:

1.

2.

3.

4.

5.

All human beings are able to think more rationally when they are calm. On the flip side, it is more difficult for anyone to think rationally when they are "worked up" or have a "button pushed." So, it makes sense that these are the times our emotions often get the best of us and we make choices that are counterproductive. Wouldn't it be nice if we could think as rationally in the "heat of the moment" as we are able to after we calm down? The reality is that most people have difficulty thinking clearly under pressure. One tool that can assist us in doing better "in the heat of the moment" is flashcards. Coping cards are designed to help us *act* differently in such moments. Cognitive cue cards are designed to help us *think* differently in those situations. The idea is, in your calm moments, write down on a 3x5 note card what you believe you need to hear during the less-calm moments.

Example

When I'm tempted to ___*gossip*___ (behavior from Tool 4),

I can (choices from Tool 6):

1. *Call a friend to vent*

2. *Journal my thoughts*

3. *Go for a walk (and leave my cell phone at home!)*

Your Coping Card

When I'm tempted to _____ (behavior from Tool 4),

I can (choices from Tool 6):

1. _____

2. _____

3. _____

A cognitive cue card does not list behaviors; rather, it takes triggers (Tool 1) and robs them of the negative meaning your critical voice is attempting to give them. Cue cards take the following form:

Example

Cognitive Cue Card

Just because *I am angry at her* **doesn't mean** *I have no self-control. I can*

chose to act consistent with my recovery.

I know *I have shown self-control in* **is true because** *I can also restrain my*
areas this week

impulse toward her.

Your Cognitive Cue Card

Cognitive Cue Card

Just because _____ **doesn't mean** _____

_____

I know _____ **is true because** _____

_____

CONCLUSION

Cognitive Behavioral Therapy (CBT) is the most empirically supported form of treatment for most psychological conditions. It has been proven to be helpful for dealing with a wide variety of problems. CBT is heavily reliant on a strong therapeutic alliance between the therapist and client. It also has a strong psychoeducational component and depends significantly on between-session work to attain goals that are concrete and measurable. Attainment of these goals is enhanced by completing homework assignments. Similar to working with a personal trainer or dietitian, goals can't be attained without between-session application and practice of the principles being learned. CBT makes no attempt to hide how people change. In this way, clients are empowered to play a collaborative role in their recovery. I have developed these "tools" as a template that can be adapted for a variety of issues ranging from severe clinical depression and anxiety disorders to self-help concerns such as codependency and low self-esteem.

Much CBT literature exists. Clinical texts, journal articles, and treatment manuals written by the brightest minds in the field for specific issues are plentiful. There are also seemingly endless workbooks that incorporate "CBT skills" with handouts, worksheets, and group activities. These often tend to be vague, random, scattered, and sometimes even too generic to be helpful. The most consistent piece of feedback I receive while presenting at workshops and seminars around the country is some version of, "I wish I had all these exercises in one place where I could find them easily." This toolbox is an attempt to do just that: to provide clinically useful exercises to facilitate continuity in treatment between sessions and for a wide range of issues. So, if you are a professional looking for a user-friendly yet theoretically sound resource, I hope you'll find this book helpful in working with clients, and if you are a client struggling with one of these issues yourself, my hope is that these tools will prove helpful as you navigate your road to recovery.

Antony, M. (2008). *The anti-anxiety handbook.* New York: Guilford Press.

Antony, M. (2009). *When perfect isn't good enough.* Oakland, CA: New Harbinger Publications.

Beattie, M. (1986) *Codependent no more.* Center City, MN: Hazelden Foundation.

Beck, A. (1987). *Cognitive therapy of depression.* New York: Guilford Press.

Beck, A. (2000). *Prisoners of hate: The cognitive basics of anger, hostility, and violence.* New York: Harper-Collins.

Beck, A. & Clark, D. (2011). *The anxiety and worry workbook: The cognitive behavioral solution.* New York: Guilford Press.

Beck, J. (2011). *Cognitive therapy: basics & beyond (second edition).* New York: Guilford Press.

Beck, J. (2005). *Cognitive therapy for challenging problems.* New York: Guilford Press.

Burns, D. (1999). *The feeling good handbook.* New York: Plume.

Cloud, H. & Townsend, J. (2002). *Boundaries: when to say yes, how to say no to take control of your life.* Grand Rapids, MI: Zondervan.

DiClemente, C.. C., et al. (2004). *Substance abuse treatment and the stages of change: selecting and planning interventions.* New York: Guilford Press.

Ellis, A. (1975). *A new guide to rational living.* New York: Wilshire Book Co.

Gates, A. & Baker, C. (1995). *The road to recovery.* Stillwater, OK: New Forums Press.

Hayes, S. (2005). *Get out of your mind and into your life: the new acceptance and commitment therapy.* Oakland, CA: New Harbinger Publications.

Leahy, B. (2003). *Cognitive therapy techniques: a practitioner's guide.* New York: Guilford Press.

Leahy, B. (2003). *Overcoming resistance in cognitive therapy.* New York: Three Rivers Press.

Leahy, B. (2006). *The worry cure: seven steps to stop worry from stopping you.* New York: Three Rivers Press.

Linehan, M. (1993). *Cognitive behavioral treatment of borderline personality disorder.* New York: Guilford Press.

Linehan, M. (1993). *Cognitive behavioral treatment of borderline personality disorder skills training manual.* New York: Guilford Press.

Linehan, M, et al. (1983). Reasons for staying alive when you are thinking of killing yourself: the Reasons for Living Inventory. *Journal of Consulting and Clinical Psychology, 51,* 276–286.

Maxwell, J. (2007). *Failing forward: turning mistakes into stepping stones for success.* Nashville, TN: Thomas Nelson Press.

Navoco, R. (2007). *Anger dysregulation*. In T. A. Cavell & K. T. Malcolm (eds). Anger, aggressions, and interventions for interpersonal violence (pp 3–54). Florence, KY: Routledge Books.

Sokol, L. & Fox, M. (2009). *Think confident, be confident*. New York: Perigee Trade.

Warren, R. (2011). *The purpose driven life*. Grand Rapids, MI: Zondervan.

Weisenheimer, D. (1985). *The anger workout book: step by step methods for greater productivity, better relationships and a healthier life*. New York: William Morrow and Co.

Wells, A. (2011). *Metacognitive therapy for anxiety and depression*. New York; Guilford Press.

Young, J. (1993) *Schema therapy: a practitioner's guide*. New York: Guilford Press.

For your convenience, we have established a dedicated website to download all the worksheets, exercises and handouts. This gives you a choice to photocopy from the book or printing. The handouts will all be labeled with the corresponding titles and pages.

go.pesi.com/riggenbach